Paper Crafts
Gourmet

a *Paper Crafts* publication

Editor-in-Chief Stacy Croninger
Managing Editor Kimberly Carroll
Creative Editor Cath Edvalson
Senior Editor Brandy Jesperson
Associate Creative Editor Megan Hoeppner
Associate Editor P. Kelly Smith
Contributing Editors Elizabeth B. Jensen, Shelisa Loertscher, Connie Myers, Nicole Snow, Emily Cannon
Copy Editor Shelisa Loertscher
Editorial Assistant Brenda Peterson
Art Director Stace Hasegawa
Designer Celeste Rockwood-Jones
Photography American Color
Production Tom Stuber, Dana Wilson

CK Media, LLC
Chief Executive Officer David O'Neil
Group Publisher/Quilting Tina Battock
VP/Editorial Director Lin Sorenson
VP/Business Development Andrew Johnson
VP/Consumer Marketing Director Susan DuBois
Circulation Director Nicole Martin
VP/Director of Events Paula Kraemer

OFFICES
Paper Crafts magazine
14850 Pony Express Rd., Bluffdale, UT 84065-4801
Ph: 801/816-8300 **Fax:** 801/816-8301
Web site *www.PaperCraftsMag.com*

Contents

Appetizers p. 7

Make your guests feel welcome with delicious appetizers. You'll have nearly as much fun preparing as you will at the party with these fabulous invitations, favors, and decorations.

Beverages p. 31

No conversation is complete without something to sip, whether it's a sophisticated pomegranatini or a nostalgic mug of hot buttered cider. So, gather your loved ones for a friendly chat or a unique party and enjoy these delightful drinks and playful projects.

Breads p. 43

There's nothing quite as mouthwatering and heart-warming as the scent of fresh-baked bread. Breads, whether in loaves, rolls, biscuits, or sweet dessert slices, add that perfect finishing touch to a meal. Add lovely paper-crafted touches of your own with these bread wraps, bags, and parties.

Desserts p. 69

What's not to love about desserts? After all, whether they're eaten as part of a meal or as a special stand-alone treat, they're always delicious. And, not only are these scrumptious paper-crafted projects calorie free, they're sure to make eating these desserts even more enjoyable. So, go on, dig in to these tasty delights and start celebrating the joy of living.

Main Dishes p. 99

From parties and place settings, to a thoughtful card and meal for someone who could use a helping hand, you'll find great paper-crafting projects to go with this selection of main dish recipes.

Snacks p. 123

Wrap up yummy snacks for after school, a hike, or a long trip with these bag toppers, boxes, tins, and more. There's even a plate that little ones can decorate and fill with Santa's cookies.

Soups p. 141

Warm up the hearts of your loved ones with these hot and savory homemade soups and stews, and coordinating paper-crafted projects. Whether you're making these tasty meals and pretty projects for a wintry day, a Sunday dinner, to give away, or simply to feed your own family, they're sure to bring a smile to your friends and loved ones' faces.

Miscellaneous p. 161

Whip up sauces, mixes, and more with fresh, fun packaging to indulge your family and friends.

5 STEPS For quick & easy projects in 5 steps or less, look for this icon throughout the book.

What's not to like about food? It helps you celebrate, comforts you when you are sick, fills cravings, and more. When asked my favorite food, I quickly answer "raviolis," of any variety. But honestly, there are few foods I don't enjoy, which is a problem when it comes to buying new clothes. Not only do I enjoy eating; I find pleasure in cooking. Whether it is a new recipe or one that is tried and true, the creation process is fun.

I also enjoy sharing what I make with others, which is one of the reasons I love this book. So many of the recipes are perfect for sharing, whether at a party, for a new baby, when someone is sick, or just to say "I'm thinking of you". Plus, we've paired these yummy recipes with creative paper-crafted projects. You'll find tags for jars of soup, wraps for loaves of bread, and party ensembles for large and small groups, plus many more ideas.

I hope you enjoy these delicious recipes and great ideas for adding paper-crafted projects to your food items. And be assured, we taste tested each recipe, so you can feel safe sharing them with those you love. (Ah, the sacrifices we make for our readers!)

Have fun cooking and creating!

StacyC

Now that you have all these wonderful recipes, you need a way to store them. Here's an easy recipe box with dividers that looks as good as the recipes taste.

5 STEPS Simply Floral Recipe Box

Designer: Stacy Croninger

1. Spell "Recipes" with rub-ons.
2. Apply flourishes to box front. Apply circles to name plate.
3. Cut patterned paper for dividers. Punch circles from cardstock; cut in half, write recipe category, and staple to divider. Repeat for each divider. Embellish with stickers.

SUPPLIES: *Cardstock:* (brown) Bazzill Basics Paper *Patterned paper:* (Fennel, Coriander, Dill Seed from Dill Blossom collection) SEI *Color medium:* (black pen) American Crafts *Accents:* (staples) *Rub-ons:* (alphabet) Creative Imaginations; (All Mixed Up alphabet) Doodlebug Design; (circles, flourishes) Stampin' Up! *Stickers:* (assorted epoxy) SEI *Tool:* (1" circle punch) Marvy Uchida *Other:* (box) We R Memory Keepers **Finished size: recipe box 6¾" x 4½" x 7", dividers 6" x 4"**

M ake your guests feel welcome with delicious appetizers. You'll have nearly as much fun preparing as you will at the party with these fabulous invitations, favors, and decorations.

APPETIZERS

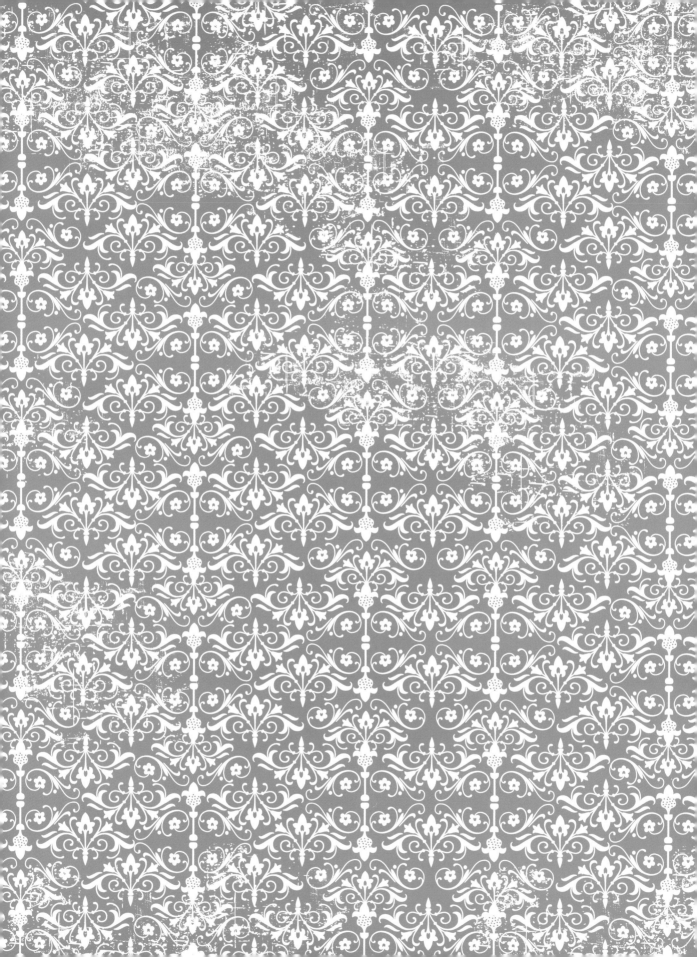

Grandma Brian's Cheese Ball Kathy Lee Garrett

This recipe is actually from my parents' neighbor's mother, hence the name "Grandma Brian's Cheese Ball." I named it that so I'd remember her and why I like it. My family loves this cheese ball, especially my husband.

INGREDIENTS

2 pkgs. (8 oz.) cream cheese
1 can (20 oz.) crushed pineapple
½ c. chopped green pepper
2 tbsp. chopped green onion
1 tbsp. Lawry's season salt

DIRECTIONS Allow cream cheese to soften on counter for an hour. Drain crushed pineapple thoroughly, using paper towels to absorb last drops of moisture. Combine all ingredients; mix with electric mixer. Line a small food storage container with clear plastic wrap (cheese ball will take on container's shape); put cheese mixture in and cover with plastic wrap. Refrigerate overnight. Optional: Roll in nuts before serving.

SUPPLIES: *Cardstock:* (blue, green, purple, black, red, yellow, white) *Patterned paper:* (Pash from Beloved collection, Puck from Wild Woodland collection) Tinkering Ink *Specialty paper:* (Night Games velvet) SEI *Rubber stamp:* (circle stitch from In Stitches set) Inque Boutique *Dye ink:* (Black) Inque Boutique *Digital elements:* (flag epoxy from Speedy kit) www.designerdigitals.com *Stickers:* (Tall Oversize alphabet) Die Cuts With a View *Fibers:* (black dotted, black/white checked ribbon) *Font:* (Hot Rod Gang BV) www.fontspace.com *Software:* (photo editing) *Adhesive:* (foam tape) *Dies:* (tag, pocket) Provo Craft *Tools:* (oval, circle cutters) Creative Memories; (die cut machine) Provo Craft *Other:* (toothpicks, thumb tacks) **Finished sizes: invitation 3¾" x 5¾", food picks 1½" x 2¾", banner 50" x 7"**

⁵ₛₜₑₚₛ Nascar Party   Designer: Betsy Veldman

INVITATION ❶ Die-cut tag and pocket from cardstock. ❷ Cut patterned paper slightly smaller than pocket front; adhere. ❸ Cut oval from cardstock; adhere and stitch. ❹ Print title on cardstock; cut into oval. Adhere and stitch. Adhere pocket closed. ❺ Open flag epoxy in software, resize as desired, and print twice on cardstock. Cut out and adhere one to pocket with foam tape. ❻ Print party information on cardstock; adhere to tag. Adhere patterned paper strips, cardstock oval, and flag epoxy. Tie with ribbon.

FOOD PICKS Print several small flag epoxies on cardstock and cut out; adhere to toothpicks.

BANNER ❶ Cut out large and small flags. Adhere together; affix letter stickers. ❷ Stamp circle stitch on cardstock; cut into strips and adhere to flags. ❸ Fold top edge of flags and adhere to ribbon, overlapping flags slightly. ❹ Open flag epoxy in software, resize as desired, and print two large and eight small on cardstock. Cut out and adhere to banner with foam tape. *Note: Adhere two small flag epoxies to thumbtacks for hanging banner.*

① Place cheese ball on plate; wrap plate and cheese ball with cellophane, tie with ribbon, and trim excess cellophane. ② Print sentiment on cardstock. Trim into tag and ink edges.

③ Adhere patterned paper and cardstock strips; stitch. Cut flower and leaf from patterned paper; adhere. ④ Punch hole in tag; affix sticker. ⑤ Attach tag to ribbon.

SUPPLIES: *Cardstock:* (navy, white) *Patterned paper:* (Beacon Hill, Spectator Cadet from Provincial Fare collection) Tinkering Ink *Dye ink:* (Night of Navy) Stampin' Up! *Sticker:* (hole reinforcer) *Fibers:* (navy organdy, grosgrain ribbon) Offray *Font:* (Palace Script SemiBold) www.fonts.com *Template:* (tag) Provo Craft *Other:* (white plate, cellophane wrap) **Finished size: 5¼" x 2½"**

Bacon Wrapped Water Chestnuts Tammy Olsen

This appetizer is great for family reunions and Christmas parties. Not only is it quick and easy to make, but it also fills the house with the delicious aroma of barbecue sauce and mouth-watering bacon.

INGREDIENTS

2 cans whole water chestnuts
1 pkg. bacon slices, cut into thirds
Barbecue sauce

DIRECTIONS Wrap chestnuts with bacon and secure with toothpicks. Bake in 9" x 13" pan at 350 degrees for 25 minutes. Drain grease. Cover chestnuts with barbecue sauce and bake an additional 20 minutes.

INVITATION ❶ Make card from cardstock. ❷ Adhere patterned paper pieces. ❸ Punch square from patterned paper; adhere beads/glitter and let dry. Adhere to card. ❹ Punch circle from patterned paper; apply red dragon rub-on to circle. Adhere with foam tape. ❺ Knot ribbon around card flap. ❻ Spell "A party" on patterned paper with rub-ons; trim, mat with cardstock, and adhere with foam tape.

CHOPSTICK WRAP ❶ Cut two 2¼" x 5½" pieces of cardstock. Stitch around three sides to create pocket. ❷ Adhere patterned paper. ❸ Punch square from patterned paper; adhere beads/glitter and let dry. Adhere to wrap. ❹ Punch circle from patterned paper; apply dragon rub-on and adhere with foam tape. ❺ Knot ribbon around wrap. Insert chopsticks.

FAVOR BOX ❶ Adhere patterned paper pieces to box. ❷ Punch square from patterned paper; adhere beads/glitter and let dry. Adhere to box. ❸ Punch circle from patterned paper; apply dragon rub-on and adhere to box with foam tape. ❹ Knot ribbon around box. ❺ Fill box with fortune cookies.

SUPPLIES: *Cardstock:* (black) *Patterned paper:* (Red/Black Alphabet, Asian Lanterns Shimmer, White Dragons from the Welcome to Asia collection) Far and Away Scrapbooks *Accents:* (gold beads/glitter) Provo Craft *Rub-ons:* (black, red dragons; Big Black alphabet) Far and Away Scrapbooks *Fibers:* (black printed ribbon) Far and Away Scrapbooks *Adhesive:* (decoupage) Plaid; (foam tape) Making Memories *Tools:* (1¼" circle punch) McGill; (1⅛" circle punch) EK Success; (1⅜" square punch) Marvy Uchida; (1¾" square punch) *Other:* (black take-out box) Westrim Crafts; (chopsticks, fortune cookies)
Finished sizes: invitation 5½" square, chopstick wraps 2¼" x 5½", favor box 4" x 4" x 4"

SUPPLIES: *Specialty paper:* (photo) *Digital elements:* (black medallion, red patterned paper, circle frame, black rickrack from Story Time kit; flourishes from On the Edge Flourishes No. 01 kit) www.designerdigitals.com; (silver brads from The Simple Florist kit, corded bookplate from Urban Bohemian kit) www.jenwilsondesigns.com; (wax seal from Wax Seal Alpha kit) www.storeide.se/gunhild/index.htm *Stickers:* (striped tape) 7gypsies *Fonts:* (Verdana, Georgia) www.myfonts.com *Software:* (photo editing) Adobe *Other:* (album, digital photos) **Finished sizes: invitation 4" x 6", card 8" square, album 9¾" x 8¾", layout 8" x 8"**

Retirement Party

Designer: Stefanie Hamilton

INVITATION ❶ Create finished size project in software; open digital elements. ❷ Drag patterned paper onto project. Cut and paste patterned paper rectangle; add drop shadow. ❸ Create new 3" x 5" project, drag onto project, and add drop shadow. ❹ Type invitation text. ❺ Drop in flourish; copy, invert, and drop in place. ❻ Drop in wax seal. Print on photo paper and trim.

CARD ❶ Create finished size project in software; open digital elements. ❷ Drag patterned paper onto project; color edges black. ❸ Create new project, change color to cream, and drag onto project. Cut and paste patterned paper rectangle. ❹ Drop in circle frame; fill with cream and type sentiment. ❺ Print on photo paper; trim. ❻ Cut cardstock to 11" x 8"; score left edge at 3" and fold. Adhere printed piece to flap to form card.

ALBUM COVER ❶ Create 6" x 8" project in software; open digital elements. ❷ Cut and paste patterned paper. Drop in rickrack. ❸ Drop in corded bookplate; type title. ❹ Print on photo paper; trim. ❺ Affix tape along album edge. Adhere printed piece and affix tape to seam.

LAYOUT ❶ Create finished size project in software; open digital elements. ❷ Change project color to black. Cut and paste patterned paper. ❸ Create 4" x 5¾" project, change color to black, and drop in photos. Drag onto project. ❹ Create text, drag onto project. ❺ Drop in brads; resize as desired. ❻ Print on photo paper, trim, and insert in album.

Inside

Annie's Fruit Salsa and Cinnamon Chips Courtesy of AllRecipes.com

This delicious salsa, made with fresh kiwis, apples, and berries, is a sweet treat when served on homemade cinnamon tortilla chips. Enjoy it as a summer appetizer or an easy dessert.

INGREDIENTS

2 kiwis, peeled and diced
2 Golden Delicious apples, peeled, cored, and diced
8 oz. raspberries
1 lb. strawberries
2 tbsp. white sugar
1 tbsp. brown sugar
3 tbsp. fruit preserves, any flavor
10 (10") flour tortillas
Butter-flavored cooking spray
2 c. cinnamon sugar

DIRECTIONS In a large bowl, thoroughly mix kiwis, apples, raspberries, strawberries, white sugar, brown sugar, and fruit preserves. Cover and chill in refrigerator at least 15 minutes. Preheat oven to 350 degrees. Coat one side of each tortilla with cooking spray. Cut tortillas into wedges and arrange in a single layer on large baking sheet. Sprinkle with cinnamon sugar. Spray again with cooking spray. Bake 8 to 10 minutes. Allow to cool 15 minutes. Serve with chilled fruit salsa.

Paper Crafts Gourmet   **13**

SUPPLIES: *Cardstock:* (Kiwi) WorldWin; (aqua, dark blue) Die Cuts With a View; (aqua) Bazzill Basics Paper *Patterned paper:* (Belleville Stripes) Scenic Route *Chalk ink:* (Blue Lagoon) Clearsnap *Accents:* (green brads) Making Memories *Fibers:* (white grosgrain ribbon) Stampin' Up! *Dies:* (Vowel Play alphabet) Ellison *Tools:* (die cut machine) Ellison; (1½", 2", 2½", 3¾" circle punches) *Other:* (gift bag) Hallmark; (water bottle) **Finished sizes: card 4" x 8½", water bottle wrap 9¼" x 3", gift bag 10" x 13"**

Pool Party Designer: Nicole Keller

LIFE PRESERVERS ❶ Punch life preserver circles from cardstock. *Note: Make one large and three small life preservers.* ❷ Cut 4 large and 12 small accent pieces from cardstock. Ink edges and adhere to life preservers. ❸ Embellish large life preserver with white ribbon.

CARD ❶ Make card from cardstock. ❷ Cut strip of patterned paper; adhere and zigzag-stitch. ❸ Adhere small life preserver. ❹ Die-cut sentiment; adhere.

WATER BOTTLE WRAP ❶ Cut cardstock to fit around water bottle and conceal label. ❷ Adhere patterned paper strips;

zigzag-stitch seams. ❸ Die-cut letters of guest's name; adhere. ❹ Adhere wrap to water bottle. Place small life preserver over neck of bottle.

GIFT BAG ❶ Cut cardstock 7½" x 12". ❷ Adhere patterned paper strips; zigzag-stitch inside and outside edges. ❸ Adhere cardstock strips. Attach brads and adhere piece to gift bag. ❹ Adhere large and small life preservers. ❺ Die-cut "Take a dip!"; adhere. ❻ Trim handles from gift bag.

BAG TOPPER ❶ Stamp French Script backgrounder, branch, and sentiment on cardstock; trim and ink edges. ❷ Die-cut scalloped rectangle from cardstock; ink edges. Adhere stamped block to rectangle, stitch, and attach brad. ❸ Make topper from patterned paper. Adhere patterned paper strip. ❹ Punch holes through front and back of topper. Set eyelets in front. ❺ Place topper over bag; poke holes in bag through eyelets. Thread ribbon through eyelets and tie.

JAR BAND ❶ Cut patterned paper to fit around jar. Adhere patterned paper strip, zigzag-stitch edge, and ink edges. ❷ Stamp French Script background and strawberry on cardstock; trim and ink edges. ❸ Die-cut scalloped rectangle from patterned paper; adhere stamped block. Stitch edges. ❹ Tie ribbon through button; adhere flower and button. ❺ Adhere rectangle to band; adhere band around jar.

SUPPLIES: *Cardstock:* (Blush Red Light, Natural Smooth) Prism *Patterned paper:* (Girl Floral, Love Stripes from Party collection) My Mind's Eye *Rubber stamps:* (sentiment, branch from Nature's Silhouettes set; French Script Backgrounder; strawberry from Sweet Thang set) Cornish Heritage Farms *Dye ink:* (Antique Linen, Juniper) Ranger Industries; (white) *Specialty ink:* (Noir hybrid) Stewart Superior Corp. *Color medium:* (Rose Red, Old Olive markers) Stampin' Up! *Accents:* (green button) Autumn Leaves; (copper brad) Making Memories; (white velvet flower) Maya Road; (white eyelets) *Fibers:* (pink gingham ribbon) Stampin' Up! *Die:* (scalloped rectangle) Spellbinders *Tools:* (die cut machine) Provo Craft; (⅛" circle punch) **Finished sizes: bag topper 5" x 3", jar band 12" x 2¾"**

Dolisca's Hummus Cath Edvalson

My sister-in-law, Dolisca, is Lebanese. Her hummus is so good and so authentic that whenever I have hummus now, I'm always comparing it to hers. Poor girl, though—whenever we have a family gathering, we ask her to bring it. I hope she doesn't get too tired of making it, because we sure don't get tired of eating it!

INGREDIENTS

½ tbsp. salt
4 tbsp. olive oil
¾ c. lemon juice
½ c. tahini
3 cans chick peas
2 large cloves garlic
4 tbsp. water
Parlsey (optional)

DIRECTIONS Place all ingredients except water in a food processor; pulse until ingredients are mixed, but not smooth. Add one tbsp. of water at a time until mixture is of desired consistency. Do not over mix.

Place in a bowl and drizzle a little olive oil on top; decorate with parsley if desired. Serve with white pita bread.

INVITATION ① Cut invitation from cardstock using template; fold and sand. ② Stamp large paisley. ③ Stamp borders; emboss. ④ Stamp large medallion on cardstock; emboss. Trim and adhere. ⑤ Cut shank from button; adhere. ⑥ Print "Book club" on cardstock. Cut to fit inside invitation using template; adhere.

BOOKMARK HOLDER ① Make bookmark from cardstock; punch two half-circles at top. Punch slit 1" from center top. ② Cut cardstock slightly smaller than bookmark; sand. Stamp large paisley; adhere. *Note: Allow slit tab to remain free on back of bookmark.* ③ Print quote on cardstock; trim and attach to bookmark with brads.

BOOKMARK ① Ink tag. Stamp dotted circle medallion; emboss. ② Punch hole in tag; attach jump ring and charm. ③ Cut 12" of cord; knot end through tag. String beads; knot. ④ Knot cord 7¼" from beaded end. String beads, knot, and trim excess cord. ⑤ Fold cord in half; slide center under quote and loop snugly around slit punch on back of bookmark.

SUPPLIES: *Cardstock:* (Ocean, Honey, Grey Wool) Close To My Heart *Clear stamps:* (large medallion, thin border from Alfresco set; large paisley, dotted circle medallion, wide border from Adorable set) Close To My Heart *Dye ink:* (Ocean, Honey) Close To My Heart *Watermark ink:* Tsukineko *Embossing powder:* (Silver) Close To My Heart *Accents:* (silver button) Blumenthal Lansing; (glass beads, silver charm) Blue Moon Beads; (silver beads, jump ring) Darice; (metal-rimmed tag) Avery; (silver brads) *Fibers:* (black elastic cord) *Fonts:* (Dragon Normal) www.bayfonts.com; (Times New Roman) Microsoft *Template:* (file folder) Provo Craft *Tools:* (slit punch, ⅛" circle punch) **Finished sizes: invitation 4½" x 6", bookmark holder 2¾" x 5¾", bookmark 1¼" x 11½"**

New Nest Jar & Tag Designer: Jessica Witty

① Cut patterned paper to fit jar; adhere. ② Cut tag from cardstock. Cut patterned paper strip, fold, and adhere to tag. ③ Stamp bird on cardstock; shade using water brush. Trim and adhere. ④ Stamp sentiment on cardstock; trim and adhere. Write "for your" with pen. ⑤ Stamp nest on cardstock; trim, shape, and adhere using foam tape. ⑥ Thread ribbon through tag; tie around jar lid.

SUPPLIES: *Cardstock:* (Close to Cocoa, kraft, white) Stampin' Up! *Patterned paper:* (Grateful Tree Farm, Grateful Multi Stripe) KI Memories *Rubber stamps:* (bird, nest, sentiment from Pretty Birds set) Cornish Heritage Farms *Chalk ink:* (Dark Brown, Blue Lagoon) Clearsnap *Color medium:* (brown pen) *Fibers:* (brown gingham ribbon) *Adhesive:* (foam tape) *Tool:* (water brush) *Other:* (glass jar) The Container Store **Finished sizes: jar 4" diameter x 5½" height, tag 2¾" x 3¼"**

Party Caprese Neko Carrillo

My mother-in-law taught me to make Caprese when I first met my husband. It is so yummy, easy to make, and best of all, looks so pretty. This dish will dress up any occasion.

INGREDIENTS

4 vine-ripe tomatoes
1 lb. fresh mozzarella
1 bunch fresh basil
Extra-virgin olive oil
Coarse salt and pepper

DIRECTIONS Cut tomatoes and mozzarella in ¼" slices. Layer alternating slices of tomato and mozzarella, adding a basil leaf between each. Drizzle with olive oil; season with salt and pepper to taste.

SUPPLIES: *Cardstock:* (white) *Patterned Paper:* (Tokyo, High Rise, Sushi Bar, Gallery, Museum, Marquee from Metropolitan collection) American Crafts *Accent:* (chipboard line) American Crafts *Rub-ons:* (Portobello alphabet) 7gypsies; (celebrate) Making Memories *Stickers:* (Jewelry Box alphabet) American Crafts *Fibers:* (black striped ribbon) *Adhesive:* (decoupage) Plaid *Tool:* (corner rounder punch) *Other:* (candle, paper mache box) **Finished sizes: invitation 5½" x 4¾", candle 3" diameter x 6" height, favor box 3" diameter x 1½" height**

Celebrate Summer Party
Designer: Wendy Sue Anderson

INVITATION ❶ Make card from cardstock; cut ½" from front flap. ❷ Adhere patterned paper strip to inside edge of card. ❸ Adhere patterned paper strip. Cut patterned paper rectangle, stitch edges, and adhere to card. *Note: Leave a section of piece unattached at top so sentiment block can wrap over the edge.* ❹ Cut patterned paper rectangle; fold and round corners. Apply rub-ons. Tie with ribbon and slide over stitched piece; adhere. ❺ Affix stickers and adhere chipboard line.

CANDLE ❶ Cut patterned paper strips to fit around candle; adhere. ❷ Adhere ribbon around seam; tie knot.

FAVOR BOX ❶ Adhere patterned paper to box sides. ❷ Cut patterned paper to fit lid; adhere and sand edges. ❸ Adhere patterned paper strip to lip of lid. ❹ Adhere ribbon to lip of lid; knot ribbon and adhere.

PREPARATION Ink and emboss all brads.

CIRCLE ACCENTS ❶ Punch circles from patterned paper; ink edges. ❷ Adhere jumbo flower brads. ❸ Punch snowflakes from patterned paper; adhere. Accent centers with glitter glue.

INVITATION ❶ Make tri-fold card from patterned paper; ink edges. ❷ Tie ribbon around invitation. ❸ Adhere circle accents.

CENTERPIECE CANDLE Attach circle accents to candle with brad prongs.

CENTERPIECE BASE ❶ Paint tin white; add glitter to wet paint on lid. ❷ Adhere patterned paper to tin sides.

❸ Adhere patterned paper circle to lid. ❹ Adhere ribbon around lip of lid. Tie ribbon around tin. ❺ Attach mini flower brads to felt snowflakes; adhere. ❻ Set candle in center of lid. Cut off long stem on berry sprigs; bend into wreath shape and place around candle.

FAVOR ❶ Paint box. Adhere ribbon around lip of lid. ❷ Cut patterned paper to fit top; ink edges and adhere. ❸ Adhere patterned paper strip around box. ❹ Attach jumbo brad to two felt snowflakes; adhere. ❺ Attach mini flower brad to felt snowflake; adhere.

SUPPLIES: *Patterned paper:* (Glee, Peppermint, Festive from Figgy Pudding collection) Basic Grey; (Shimmer Snowball Stripe from Snowday collection) Paper Salon *Pigment ink:* (white) Stampin' Up! *Chalk ink:* (brown) Clearsnap *Embossing powder:* (Turquoise glitter) Ranger Industries *Paint:* (white) Delta *Accents:* (white felt snowflakes) CPE, Inc.; (jumbo, mini flower brads; jumbo brad) Queen & Co.; (iridescent glitter glue) Ranger Industries; (clear glitter) FloraCraft *Fibers:* (red velvet, red organza ribbon) Michaels *Tools:* (snowflake punch) Marvy Uchida; (1½" circle punch) *Other:* (glittered candle, berry sprigs, cookie tin, box) **Finished sizes: invitation 4¼" x 5½", centerpiece candle 3" diameter x 6" height, centerpiece base 7¼" diameter x 2¾" height, favor 3¼" diameter x 1¾" height**

Maria's Bruschetta Cath Edvalson

This is so good, you can't stop eating it—and you'll be wishing you'd planned it for your entire meal. My sister-in-law, Maria, makes this recipe every time we go to visit her in New Hampshire, and by the time it's time for dinner, we're so full from the bruschetta, it's hard to eat what's planned!

INGREDIENTS

4-6 Roma tomatoes
¼ red onion
1 jar (16 oz.) marinated mushrooms
1 jar (16 oz.) marinated sweet red peppers
1 small jar capers
1 handful fresh basil, chopped
⅓ c. olive oil
1 tsp. white vinegar

DIRECTIONS Chop tomatoes finely and let juices drain. Chop onion, mushrooms, and red peppers, and layer them one at a time in a glass container or jar. Additionally layer capers, basil, and tomatoes. Pour olive oil and vinegar over the ingredients and allow to marinate for a couple of hours. To serve, stir together and place on toasted French bread.

INVITATION ❶ Make card from cardstock; cut 1½" from front flap. ❷ Cover front and inside with patterned paper; ink edges. ❸ Punch edge of cardstock strip with slit punch to create scallops; adhere behind front flap. Zigzag-stitch seam. ❹ Stamp party list on cardstock; punch edge with spiral binding punch. Ink edges and adhere to card. Adhere rhinestone and attach photo turn with brad. ❺ Paint flourish; ink and adhere. Ink flower. Tie ribbon through loop brad; insert brad through flower and adhere.

FAVOR TIN ❶ Cut patterned paper to fit lid of tin; ink edges and adhere. ❷ Cut patterned paper strip to fit around tin; adhere ends to form band. ❸ Stamp sentiment circle on cardstock; punch out and ink edges. ❹ Die-cut scalloped circle from cardstock; adhere stamped circle. ❺ Punch circle from patterned paper; ink edges and adhere. ❻ Tie button with ribbon. Ink flower and adhere flower and button to band. Slide band over tin.

BINGO CARD ❶ Cut cardstock to 8" square. Adhere patterned paper strips; zigzag-stitch. ❷ Double-mat with cardstock. ❸ Have guests stamp sentiments and wedding images on their cards upon arrival based on their individual preferences.

HOW TO PLAY THE GAME

Have all your guests sit down with their bingo cards, and play the game similar to how you would a regular Bingo game. The only difference is that you'll be calling out each sentiment and wedding image. The first guest to have three called—and verified—designs in a row wins the game.

SUPPLIES: *Cardstock:* (Blush Red Light, Natural Smooth) Prism Papers; (brown) *Patterned paper:* (Paisley, Stripes from Out & About No.1 collection) My Mind's Eye *Rubber stamps:* (party list from It's a Party set; sentiment circle from Celebration Frames set; sentiments, wedding images from Gettin' Hitched set) Lizzie Anne Designs *Dye ink:* (Antique Linen, Pink Sherbet) Ranger Industries; (Regal Rose) Stampin' Up! *Paint:* (Spotlight White) Making Memories *Accents:* (peach/pink flowers) Prima; (ivory photo turn, brad) Making Memories; (chipboard flourish) Maya Road; (cream button) Autumn Leaves; (copper loop brad) Karen Foster Design; (pink rhinestone) *Fibers:* (pink velvet ribbon) May Arts; (brown stitched ribbon) *Die:* (scalloped circle) Spellbinders *Tools:* (spiral binding punch, slit punch) Stampin' Up!; (1¾", 1" circle punches) EK Success; (die cut machine) Provo Craft *Other:* (silver candy tin) Pinecone Press **Finished sizes: invitation 5¾" x 4¼", favor tin 3¾" x 2¼" x ¾", bingo card 8¾" square**

SUPPLIES: *Cardstock:* (kraft) Bazzill Basics Paper *Patterned paper:* (Winter Birds, Winter Star from Winter Garden collection) Creative Imaginations; (Learn from Color Me Silly collection) Basic Grey *Rubber stamps:* (swirl, small circle, large circle from Petals set; frame from Story Boards set) Inque Boutique *Pigment ink:* (brown) Clearsnap *Accents:* (chipboard tile) Deluxe Designs; (chipboard swirl) Fancy Pants Designs; (clear rhinestones) EK Success *Rub-ons:* (French Twist alphabet) Autumn Leaves *Fibers:* (rust grosgrain ribbon) Morex *Font:* (Porcelain) www.dafont.com *Tools:* (decorative-edge scissors) Fiskars; (¾" circle punch) **Finished sizes: tag 3" x 5", lid topper 2¾" diameter**

Bruschetta Wrap Designer: Anabelle O'Malley

TAG

Create ① Cut tag from cardstock; stitch edges. ② Ink edges of patterned paper strip; adhere. ③ Cut cardstock strip to fit right side of tag; cover with patterned paper. ④ Trim patterned paper and cardstock strips with decorative-edge scissors; ink edges and adhere to piece. Stitch edges and zigzag-stitch seam. ⑤ Adhere piece to tag; ink edges.

Embellish ① Stamp large circle on cardstock; cut out and adhere. Punch circle from cardstock; ink edges and adhere. ② Stamp swirl and small circle on patterned paper; cut out and adhere. ③ Cover chipboard tile with patterned paper; ink edges and adhere. ④ Stamp frame on patterned paper; trim. Straight-stitch edges and zigzag-stitch top. Apply rub-on and adhere. ⑤ Print "ruschetta" on cardstock; trim. Ink edges and adhere. ⑥ Cut paper loop; adhere to tag. Adhere rhinestones.

LID TOPPER

① Cut circle from patterned paper to fit lid; ink and stitch edges. ② Cover chipboard flourish with patterned paper; adhere to circle. Adhere rhinestones. ③ Adhere topper to jar lid. Thread ribbon through paper loop on tag; tie around jar.

Killer Cheese Fondue Pattie Donham

Fondue and fun times just seem to go together, and this recipe really puts a smile on everyone's faces when I serve it at a party.

INGREDIENTS

2 pkgs. (8 oz.) cream cheese, cut in chunks
1 round Brie cheese, cut in chunks
1 block Gruyere cheese, shredded
1 dark lager beer

DIRECTIONS Place cheeses in a large bowl; pour beer over cheese, stirring. Melt slowly in microwave, stirring frequently with a wooden spoon until melted. Pour into fondue pot; light flame underneath to keep warm. Serve with sour dough bread chunks, blanched broccoli, pre-cooked sausage bites, pitted dates, or Honey Crisp apples. For even more flavor, dip into fondue and then into a can of crunchy fried onions.

SUPPLIES: *Cardstock:* (black, white) Stampin' Up! *Patterned paper:* (Psychedelic, British Invasion from Amplified collection) American Crafts *Accents:* (white clip) Making Memories; (brown brad, green button) *Stickers:* (Moma alphabet; flowers, leaf, circles, photo corners) American Crafts *Fibers:* (black grosgrain ribbon, pink floss) *Tool:* (⅛" circle punch) *Other:* (white floating frame) Target; (photo) **Finished sizes: insert 4¼" x 14¾", invitation pocket 4¾" x 5", frame 11" x 11"**

Say Cheese Party Designer: Megan Hoeppner

INVITATION

Insert ❶ Cut three 4¼" x 4¾" panels from cardstock. Punch two corner holes on two panels and four corner holes on the center panel; attach panels with ribbon. ❷ Adhere cardstock squares. ❸ Affix alphabet, photo corners, and leaf stickers. ❹ Cut decorative elements from patterned paper; adhere. ❺ Tie ribbon to white clip; attach to top panel.

Pocket ❶ Cut 4¾" x 10¼" piece from patterned paper. Fold 5" from each end and adhere left edge to form pocket. ❷ Cut decorative elements from patterned paper. ❸ Affix flower stickers and adhere decorative elements. Attach brad to circle stickers; affix. ❹ Fold insert and place in pocket.

FRAME ❶ Cut decorative elements from patterned paper. ❷ Mat photo with patterned paper; adhere photos and decorative elements between layers of glass. ❸ Affix flower stickers between layers of glass. ❹ Reassemble frame; affix flower stickers to outside of glass. Stitch button with floss; adhere.

Insert

CARD ❶ Make card from cardstock. ❷ Cut patterned paper smaller than card front; mat with patterned paper and adhere. ❸ Cut circles from transparency sheet; adhere. Cut numbers from cardstock; adhere. ❹ Adhere patterned paper strip. Affix stickers.

FONDUE FORK WRAP ❶ Cut patterned paper 5" x 6", fold in thirds, and adhere in back and at bottom. ❷ Adhere strips of patterned paper. ❸ Adhere cardstock strip. ❹ Knot ribbon around wrap.

FOOD PLACE CARDS ❶ Make place cards from cardstock. ❷ Adhere strips of patterned paper and cardstock. ❸ Paint chipboard letters; let dry. Attach snaps; adhere to place cards. ❹ Affix alphabet stickers.

SUPPLIES: *Cardstock:* (Squash) Bazzill Basics Paper; (Bluebird, Hazard die cut from Pop Culture Gossip collection; Red Hot die cut from Pop Culture Hopscotch collection) KI Memories *Patterned paper:* (Surprise Napkin, Surprise Giftwrap) KI Memories; (Heather from Princess collection) CherryArte *Transparency sheet:* (Mod Circles Brown) Hambly Screen Prints *Paint:* (red) Delta *Accents:* (chipboard alphabet) Cosmo Cricket; (green, yellow, blue, orange snaps) We R Memory Keepers *Stickers:* (Sarah Script alphabet) American Crafts *Fibers:* (red polka dot ribbon) Offray **Finished sizes: card 6¾" x 5½", fondue fork wrap 2¾" x 6¼", apples place card 4½" x 3¾", bread place card 5" x 3½"**

Brie with Caramelized Shallots, Pears, & Pistachios Susan Neal

The French word for appetizer is amuse-bouche, which literally means to amuse the mouth. The contrast of flavors and texture in this mouthful fits the bill!

INGREDIENTS

¼ small Brie wheel
2 large shallots, sliced
1 tbsp. vegetable oil
¼ tbsp. butter
2 red or green Anjou pears, halved and sliced
¼ c. pistachios, chopped
Crackers

DIRECTIONS Sauté sliced shallots over medium heat; cook until caramelized and light brown. Arrange all ingredients on a serving dish. To pre-assemble, place slice of Brie on cracker. Top with slice of pear, shallots, and pistachios.

INVITATION ❶ Cut cardstock to finished size. Adhere cardstock strips. ❷ Print invitation details on cardstock; trim. Stamp Eiffel tower; ink edges. ❸ Adhere invitation to base with foam tape.

NAPKINS Stamp Eiffel tower and stars; let dry.

FOOD PICKS ❶ Cut cardstock to finished width; adhere cardstock strips. ❷ Trim with wave trimmer. *Note: Cut and adhere long strips, then use wave trimmer to easily cut several flags.* ❸ Adhere to toothpicks.

SUPPLIES: *Cardstock:* (White Prismatic, Classic Blue, Classic Red) Prism *Clear stamps:* (Eiffel tower from Amour Sentiments set) My Sentiments Exactly!; (star from BackRounds Large set, star from BackRounds Medium set) Technique Tuesday *Pigment ink:* (Cerulean Blue, Camellia) Tsukineko *Font:* (Paris Metro) www.dafont.com *Adhesive:* (foam tape) Therm O Web *Tool:* (wave trimmer) Creative Memories *Other:* (white napkins, toothpicks) **Finished sizes: invitation 4½" x 6", napkins 5" square, flag food picks 1½" x 2½"**

SUPPLIES: *Cardstock:* (Green Tea, Bitter Chocolate) Bazzill Basics Paper *Patterned paper:* (Green Ornament from Roam collection) K&Company *Rubber stamps:* (Pear) Stampers Anonymous *Pigment ink:* (brown) Clearsnap *Paint:* (Dark Chocolate) Delta *Finish:* (matte spray) Delta *Accents:* (copper brads) Making Memories; (fabric-covered brads) K&Company *Fibers:* (brown trim) *Fonts:* (Aramis, Porcelain) www.abstractfonts.com *Other:* (wood basket, jumbo clothespin) **Finished sizes: invitation 7" x 5", basket 10½" x 5¼" x 13¾", favor 1½" x 6" x 1¼", recipe card 4½" x 3¾"**

Easter Brunch
Designer: Susan Neal

INVITATION ❶ Make card from cardstock. ❷ Print invitation text on cardstock; trim and adhere. ❸ Cut patterned paper rectangle. Stamp Pear. Attach copper brads; ink edges and adhere. ❹ Adhere trim; attach fabric-covered brad.

BASKET ❶ Paint basket; let dry. Sand lightly; spray inside with finish. ❷ Print quote on cardstock; trim and adhere to basket side. ❸ Cut patterned paper to fit; sand and ink edges. Stamp Pear. ❹ Attach copper brads; adhere piece to basket.

FAVOR ❶ Print recipe on cardstock; mat with cardstock. ❷ Paint clothespin; let dry and sand lightly. ❸ Cut patterned paper to fit clothespin. Stamp Pear; sand and ink edges, and adhere. ❹ Adhere trim and fabric-covered brad. Attach recipe card.

No conversation is complete without something to sip, whether it's a sophisticated pomegranatini or a nostalgic mug of hot buttered cider. So, gather your loved ones for a friendly chat or a unique party and enjoy these delightful drinks and playful projects.

BEVERAGES

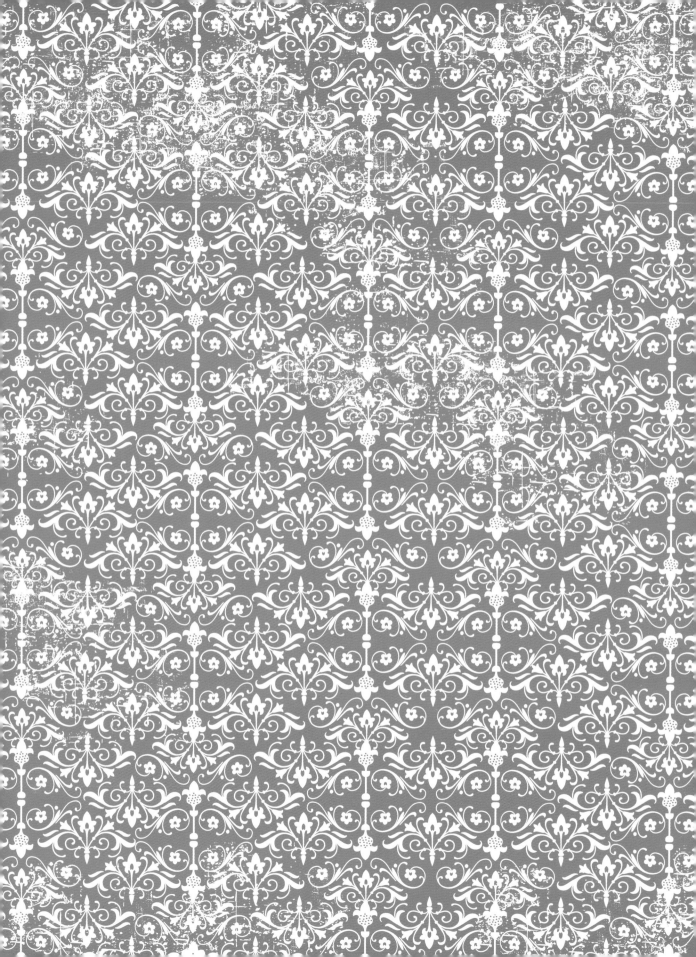

Pomegranatini Courtesy of AllRecipes.com

Dress up your party with this fun twist on the cosmopolitan, made with pomegranate juice, vodka, and orange liqueur.

INGREDIENTS

2 fluid oz. vodka
2 fluid oz. orange liqueur
2 fluid oz. pomegranate juice
1 c. crushed ice
1 twist lemon zest

DIRECTIONS Pour vodka, liqueur, and pomegranate juice in a shaker and add crushed ice. Shake vigorously; strain into glass. Garnish with twist of lemon zest.

YIELDS 1 SERVING

SUPPLIES: *Cardstock:* (red) Bazzill Basics Paper; (cream) Provo Craft *Patterned paper:* (Black Pinstripe, Leopard Chic from All Dressed Up collection) Die Cuts With a View *Rubber stamp:* (martini glass) *Dye Ink:* (red) Marvy Uchida *Accents:* (red rhinestones, red rhinestone circles) Me & My Big Ideas; (silver bead chain) Making Memories; (silver safety pin) *Fibers:* (red ribbon) May Arts *Font:* (Century Gothic) www.myfonts.com *Template:* (circle) Provo Craft *Tool:* (⅛" circle punch) *Other:* (glassine envelope) Waste Not Paper **Finished sizes: invitation 5½" x 4¾", charms 1½", favor 3" x 4½"**

⁙⁵⁙ Girls' Night In Party Designer: Teri Anderson

INVITATION ❶ Make card and card base from cardstock. ❷ Adhere patterned paper to base. ❸ Tie ribbon around base. ❹ Stamp martini glass on cardstock; cut into tag. Attach to ribbon with safety pin. ❺ Print "Girls' Night In" on cardstock. Trim, adhere, and accent with rhinestone. ❻ Adhere base to card.

CHARMS ❶ Cut small, medium, and large circles from cardstock and patterned paper using template. Layer circles and adhere. ❷ Punch hole for chain. ❸ Print sentiment on cardstock; trim and adhere. ❹ Adhere rhinestones. ❺ Thread bead chain through hole.

FAVOR ENVELOPE ❶ Cut patterned paper slightly smaller than envelope. Cut circle from piece. Adhere rectangle to envelope. ❷ Tie ribbon. ❸ Cut slightly smaller circle from patterned paper; adhere. ❹ Print and trim sentiment; adhere. ❺ Adhere rhinestones.

FAVOR INSERT ❶ Print sentiment on cardstock; ❷ Insert in envelope.

SIMPLE SENTIMENT:

DR. M'S CURES FOR OVERINDULGENCE

• Take two aspirin and go back to bed. Moan excessively about the night before and complain about your aching head.

• Suck up some sugar – chocolate and jellybeans. Some claim it works, but who cares? There's chocolate involved.

• Plan another pomegranatini rendezvous with your buddies. This one was so great. Just imagine what the next one will be like!

Congratulations Ice Bucket Wrap Designer: Alice Golden

① Cut patterned paper to finished size; adhere patterned paper. ② Cut oval from patterned paper; ink edges and apply rub-on. ③ Cut out bracket stickers. *Note: Do not remove clear backing.* Place at top and bottom of oval as a guide and trim oval to fit behind stickers. ④ Adhere oval; affix stickers. ⑤ Wrap around ice bucket.

SUPPLIES: *Patterned paper:* (striped, orange floral, green floral from Modern Milan collection) Me & My Big Ideas *Dye ink:* (Shabby Shutters) Ranger Industries *Rub-on:* (congratulations) Deja Views *Stickers:* (dreams tag, epoxy floral brackets) Me & My Big Ideas *Template:* (oval) Provo Craft **Finished size: 12" x 6¾"**

Cameron's Orange Smoothie <small>Brenda Peterson</small>

My son, Cameron, started creating smoothies when he was in seventh grade. Now he's the official smoothie maker when our family plays board games. The creamy orange flavor always reminds me of him tossing the ice cubes in the blender for us all to enjoy.

INGREDIENTS

4 oz. frozen orange juice concentrate
¼ c. milk
1 tsp. vanilla
¼ c. sugar
10-12 ice cubes

DIRECTIONS Combine all ingredients in blender. Blend until smooth. *Note: More milk can be added to achieve desired consistency.* Pour into glasses and serve.

YIELDS 2-3 SERVINGS

Little Fishy Birthday Party
Designer: Wendy Johnson

INVITATION ❶ Make card, following pattern on p. 175. *Note: Align tail on fold. Ink edges.* ❷ Cut large fins and tail, following pattern on p. 175. Ink edges; adhere. Cover tail with patterned paper. ❸ Affix sticker. Adhere cording and rickrack. ❹ Print party information on paper. Trim to fit inside card; adhere.

HAT CHARM ❶ Cut small fish and fins following patterns on p. 175. Cover tail with patterned paper. ❷ Ink edges and adhere. ❸ Attach brad; adhere cording and rickrack. ❹ Repeat for additional charms.

HAT ❶ Unfold party hat to use as pattern. Trace on patterned paper and cut out. Assemble. ❷ Adhere cording. ❸ Attach hat charm with cording. ❹ Knot ends of ribbon together. Thread through hat; adhere.

STRAW CHARMS ❶ Cut small fish and fins following pattern on p. 175. Cover tail with patterned paper. ❷ Cut patterned paper to cover back. Adhere ends only to form sleeve. Slide onto straw.

GAME SIGN & CARDS ❶ Paint skewer. ❷ Cut rectangle from patterned paper. ❸ Print game title on paper; trim and adhere. ❹ Adhere rickrack. ❺ Adhere game sign and hat charm to skewer. Place in fishbowl filled with fish crackers. ❻ Print game cards on paper.

Inside

SUPPLIES: *Paper:* (white) *Patterned paper:* (Stripe/Dot, Confetti/Green from Party Time Boy collection) Pebbles Inc. *Dye ink:* (Citrus Leaf, Sunflower) Close To My Heart *Paint:* (Honeydew) Making Memories *Accents:* (black brads) American Crafts *Sticker:* (dimensional black dot) Pebbles Inc. *Fibers:* (white rickrack) Wrights; (green ribbon) American Crafts; (blue, yellow polka dot ribbon) Michaels; (orange ribbon) Adornit-Carolee's Creations; (white cording) *Font:* (Huxtable) www.1001fonts.com *Other:* (glass fishbowl, straw, party hat, wood skewer, fish crackers) **Finished sizes: invitation 5½" x 6", hat charm 2" x 1¾", hat 4" diameter x 6" height, straw charms 4¼" x 3½", game sign 4¼" x 2¾", game cards 4¼" x 3½"**

SUPPLIES: *Cardstock:* (Deep Black, Butternut Orange, Graceful Geranium) WorldWin *Patterned paper:* (Elementary from Recess collection) BasicGrey *Chalk ink:* (Burnt Sienna, Creamy Brown) Clearsnap *Accents:* (maroon brads) Creative Impressions *Rub-ons:* (celebrate, good job) Making Memories *Stickers:* (Wilma alphabet) BasicGrey *Fibers:* (black ribbon) *Font:* (Broadway) www.fonts.com *Adhesive:* (foam tape) *Tools:* (2½" circle, scalloped circle punches) Marvy Uchida *Other:* (spiral-bound album) Borders **Finished sizes: invitation 3¾" x 7¾", gift card holder 4" x 3¼", album 8½" x 6¾"**

⦚5⦚ Graduation Party Designer: Linda Beeson

CIRCLE ACCENTS ❶ Print "Congrats grad!" once and "Class of 2009" twice on patterned paper; punch. ❷ Ink edges and mat with scalloped circles punched from cardstock.

INVITATION ❶ Make card from cardstock. ❷ Ink edges of patterned paper rectangle. Mat with cardstock and adhere to card. ❸ Cut slit in card fold; thread ribbon through and tie. ❹ Attach brads to circle accent. Adhere with foam tape.

GIFT CARD HOLDER ❶ Make holder from cardstock. ❷ Adhere flap on two sides to form pocket. Apply rub-ons. ❸ Cut rectangle from patterned paper. Ink edges and mat with cardstock. Adhere to holder front. ❹ Adhere circle accent.

ALBUM ❶ Ink edges of patterned paper rectangle. ❷ Double mat with cardstock. Adhere to album. ❸ Adhere circle accent with foam tape. ❹ Affix stickers.

BONUS IDEA

Personalize the circle accents with the name of the school or the graduate.

Raspberry Sherbet Punch Wendy Gallamore

This pretty pink punch is foamy and light. While simple to prepare, it adds a fancy touch to any festivity.

INGREDIENTS

1 can (12 oz.) raspberry lemonade concentrate
2 cans cold water
½ gal. raspberry sherbet
2 bottles (2 ltr.) lemon-lime soda, chilled

DIRECTIONS

In large punch bowl, combine lemonade concentrate and water. Scoop sherbet into bowl. Pour soda on top just before serving.

YIELDS 25 SERVINGS

SUPPLIES: *Cardstock:* (Lily White) Bazzill Basics Paper *Patterned paper:* (Hillary Lace Flower from Noteworthy collection) Making Memories; (peach floral from Dollhouse collection) K&Company *Dye ink:* (Old Paper) Ranger Industries *Accents:* (label die cuts) K&Company; (green eyelets) We R Memory Keepers; (staple) *Rub-ons:* (Simply Sweet alphabet) Doodlebug Design *Stickers:* (dimensional glitter flowers, butterfly; dollhouse) K&Company; (Two Scoops alphabet) BasicGrey *Fibers:* (yellow stitched twill ribbon) BasicGrey *Die:* (scalloped frame) Provo Craft *Tools:* (die cut machine) Provo Craft; (corner rounder punch) **Finished sizes: sign 7" square, invitation 5¼" x 3¾"**

5 steps Open House Party Designer: Melissa Phillips

SIGN ❶ Die-cut scalloped frame from patterned paper; ink edges. ❷ Adhere cardstock behind frame. ❸ Adhere die cut and affix stickers. ❹ Set eyelets and thread ribbon through at both ends. Knot.

INVITATION ❶ Make invitation from cardstock. Round bottom corners. ❷ Ink edges of patterned paper rectangle; adhere. ❸ Round bottom corners of patterned paper strip; ink edges and adhere. ❹ Ink edges of die cut. Spell "Open house" with rub-ons. Staple ribbon and adhere. ❺ Affix sticker.

BONUS IDEA

Create your own dimensional glitter stickers by layering stickers, die cuts, or chipboard shapes using foam tape, then embellishing with glitter.

BABY FEET CHARMS ❶ Stamp baby feet on cardstock; punch. ❷ Punch hole in top.

INVITATION ❶ Make invitation from patterned paper. Adhere square of patterned paper; stitch edges. ❷ Die-cut scalloped square from patterned paper; adhere. ❸ Adhere label die cut. Adhere patterned paper strip; stitch. ❹ Adhere printed ribbon. Apply rub-on. ❺ Emboss flower circle on patterned paper. Punch with scallop circle. Tie baby feet charm with floss, and attach scalloped circle, flower, and charm with brad. Adhere to invitation.

FAVOR ❶ Emboss flower circle on patterned paper. Punch with scallop circle. ❷ Adhere patterned paper strip. Wrap around chocolate and adhere ends. ❸ Tie ribbon around chocolate and knot through scalloped circle, flower, and baby feet charm.

BLOCK ❶ Cut patterned paper to fit block sides; stitch edges. ❷ Die-cut scalloped squares from patterned paper; adhere to squares; stitch. Adhere to block. ❸ Stamp precious baby sentiment on block top. Adhere photos to sides. ❹ Embellish as desired.

SUPPLIES: *Cardstock:* (pink) Bazzill Basics Paper *Patterned paper:* (Audrey Pink Floral from Noteworthy collection) Making Memories; (Pink Quilt, Pink Gingham, Adorable Girl Stripe from Adorable Girl collection) Creative Imaginations; (It's a Girl News) KI Memories *Clear stamps:* (baby feet, precious baby sentiment from Baby Sentiments set) My Sentiments Exactly! *Accents:* (pink glitter brads) Creative Imaginations; (white embossed flowers) Prima; (pink felt flowers, scalloped border) Fancy Pants Designs; (label die cut) Making Memories; (pink glitter glue, pink rhinestones) *Rub-on:* (you're invited) Die Cuts With a View *Stickers:* (Adorable Girl alphabet) Creative Imaginations *Fibers:* (white printed ribbon) Creative Imaginations; (pink twill ribbon) Jo-Ann Stores; (pink floss) *Template:* (flower circle embossing) Provo Craft *Die:* (scalloped square) Provo Craft *Tools:* (die cut, embossing machine) Provo Craft; (scallop circle punch, ½" circle punch) EK Success; (⅛" circle punch) *Other:* (wood block) K&Company; (pink wrapped chocolates) Ghirardelli Chocolate; (photos) **Finished sizes: invitation 4½" square, favor 3" x 2", block 4" cube**

Hot Buttered Apple Cider Courtesy of AllRecipes.com

Maple syrup sweetens up this hot cider, while the spiced butter gives it a rich, smooth flavor that makes it a particularly soothing drink. Fill up a mug and reminisce about cold, wintry days gone by.

INGREDIENTS

1 bottle (16 oz.) apple cider
½ c. pure maple syrup
½ c. butter, softened
½ tsp. ground nutmeg
½ tsp. ground allspice

DIRECTIONS In slow cooker over low heat, cook apple cider with maple syrup for twenty minutes or until steaming. In small bowl, combine butter, nutmeg, and allspice. Mix well. Pour cider into mugs and top with a teaspoon of spiced butter.

YIELDS 8 SERVINGS

INVITATION *Ink all edges.* ❶ Cut patterned paper to finished size. ❷ Print invitation on patterned paper; trim. Stamp Trees Backgrounder; adhere. ❸ Tie ribbon through button; adhere.

CUP SLEEVE *Ink all edges.* ❶ Cut patterned paper to finished size. Stamp Polka Dots Backgrounder. ❷ Stamp mugs on patterned paper; punch and adhere. ❸ Print names on patterned paper; trim, attach brads, and adhere. ❹ Adhere sleeve ends around cup.

DESIGNER TIP

Change the size of certain letters in the text to make them stand out and add interest.

SUPPLIES: *Patterned paper:* (Marli from Sweet Spring collection) Fancy Pants Designs; (Swirls from Out & About No.2 collection) My Mind's Eye *Rubber stamps:* (mug from Hugs & Kisses set, mug from Christmas Cheer set, Trees Backgrounder, Polka Dots Backgrounder) Cornish Heritage Farms *Dye ink:* (Sky) Paper Salon *Solvent ink:* (Jet Black) Tsukineko *Accents:* (aqua brads) Creative Impressions; (aqua button) Autumn Leaves *Fibers:* (cream ribbon) Beaux Regards *Font:* (Times New Roman) Microsoft *Tools:* (1¾" circle punch) EK Success *Other:* (disposable coffee cups) **Finished sizes: invitation 4" x 5¼", cup sleeve 10¾" x 2½"**

SUPPLIES: *Cardstock:* (Totally Tan) WorldWin; (Cherry Splash, white) Bazzill Basics Paper; (silver) Die Cuts With a View *Specialty paper:* (Night Games velvet) SEI *Color medium:* (brown pen) *Stickers:* (frame, tag, Holiday Hoopla alphabet) SEI *Fibers:* (gold dotted ribbon) SEI *Font:* (Med Ved) www.signdna.com *Adhesive:* (foam tape) *Tool:* (star punch) *Other:* (burgundy wire) Artistic Wire; (kraft gift bag) **Finished sizes: invitation 4¼" x 7¾", favor bag 4" x 5¼"**

Lights On Christmas Party Designer: Kim Kesti

INVITATION ❶ Print party details on cardstock, leaving room for center embellishment. Trim and mat with cardstock. ❷ Affix frame sticker. ❸ Cut light bulb, highlight, and top from cardstock, following pattern on p. 175. Adhere. ❹ Twist wire around top. Adhere with foam tape.

FAVOR BAG ❶ Cut rectangle from velvet paper; mat with cardstock. Adhere to gift bag. ❷ Cut tag from cardstock. Affix tag and alphabet stickers. Write sentiment with brown pen. ❸ Punch star in tag with; thread wire through star and attach to handle. Tie on ribbon.

There's nothing quite as mouthwatering and heartwarming as the scent of fresh-baked bread. Breads, whether in loaves, rolls, biscuits, or sweet dessert slices, add that perfect finishing touch to a meal. Add lovely paper-crafted touches of your own with these bread wraps, bags, and parties.

BREADS

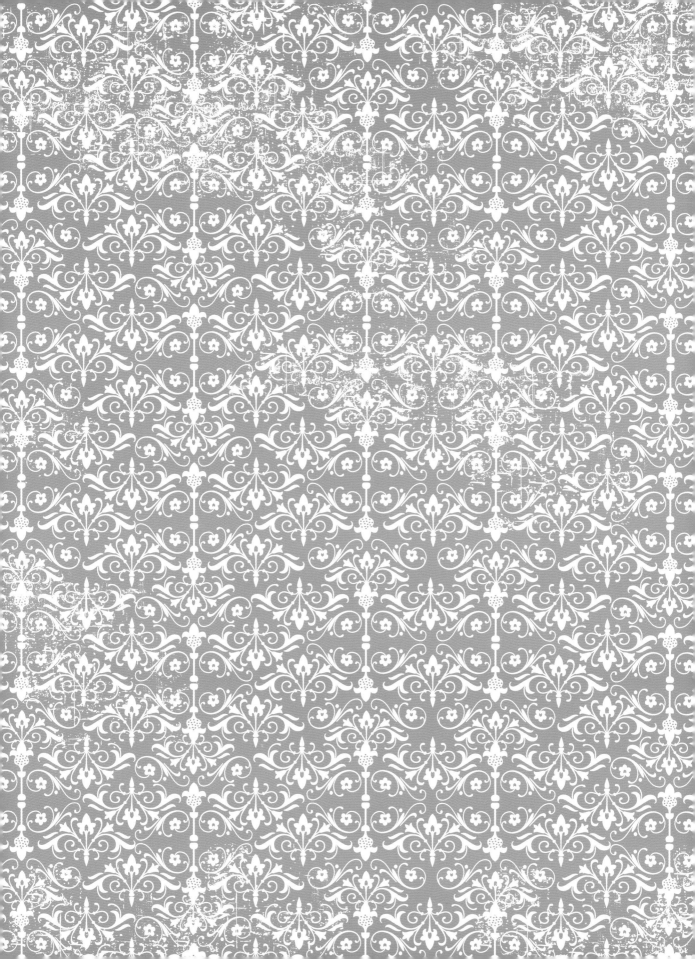

Skinny Banana Bread Stefanie Hamilton

like this recipe because it has really helped me stay on track in terms of weight during my cancer treatment. It's a great tasting treat that doesn't taste almost fat-free, and making it taught me the art of substituting healthy ingredients for high fat ingredients. Plus, everyone needs a recipe for those mushy bananas!

INGREDIENTS

¾ c. whole wheat flour
¾ c. white flour
½ c. sugar
1¼ tsp. baking powder
½ tsp. baking soda
½ tsp. nutmeg
½ tsp. cinnamon
¼ tsp salt
1 whole egg
3 bananas, mashed
⅓ - ½ c. applesauce (use more applesauce if using smaller bananas.)
⅓ c. raisins (optional)
⅓ c. walnuts (optional)

DIRECTIONS Mix dry ingredients and wet ingredients separately. Blend together very gently, just enough to moisten dry ingredients. Pour into a bread pan. Bake at 350 degrees for 55 minutes or until knife comes out clean.

SUPPLIES: *Cardstock:* (white) *Digital elements:* (blue paper, star from Re-Collections 1 kit) www.twolittlepixels.com; (scalloped border from Artsy Edged Punches kit) www.twopeasinabucket.com *Fibers:* (green stitched grosgrain ribbon) May Arts *Font:* (Verdana) Microsoft *Software:* (photo editing) Adobe
Finished size: 12" x 4"

Weigh to Go Wrap Designer: Stefanie Hamilton

① Create finished size project in software. ② Drag paper onto project. Change color of border and drop in. Flip border and drop in again. Print on cardstock and trim. ③ Create new project. Drop in star and resize. Type sentiment. Print on cardstock and trim. ④ Adhere ribbon to wrap; adhere ribbon ends around bread. ⑤ Punch hole in star piece; knot with ribbon. Adhere to wrap.

SUPPLIES: *Cardstock:* (brown) *Patterned paper:* (Baby Blossoms from Botanical Bliss collection) Tinkering Ink *Rubber stamp:* (swirl from Page Seals set) Inque Boutique *Dye ink:* (brown) *Accent:* (chipboard tag) Bazzill Basics Paper; (yellow flower) Prima; (red brad) Die Cuts With a View *Sticker:* (enjoy) Making Memories *Fibers:* (olive grosgrain ribbon) Offray *Adhesive:* (foam tape) *Die:* (wreath) Provo Craft *Tools:* (die cut machine, decorative-edge scissors) Provo Craft; (scallop circle punch) EK Success *Other:* (elastic) **Finished size: wrap 5½" x 11½"**

Enjoy Wrap   Designer: Betsy Veldman

① Cut patterned paper to finished size. Trim patterned paper strip with decorative-edge scissors; adhere. ② Cover chipboard tag with patterned paper; sand edges. ③ Die-cut wreath from cardstock; adhere to tag. ④ Punch scallop circle from patterned paper; affix sticker. Stamp swirl. Attach flower with brad; adhere to tag with foam tape. ⑤ Adhere ribbon to wrap; tie to tag. ⑥ Stitch elastic to wrap ends.

Granny's Orange Cranberry Nut Bread Alice Golden

My grandmother was a terrific cook and I got my love of cooking from her. Whenever I make this recipe I feel as though Granny is in the kitchen with me.

INGREDIENTS

2 c. flour
½ tsp. salt
1½ tsp. baking powder
½ tsp. baking soda
1 c. sugar
Zest and juice of 1 large orange
2 tbsp. oil
1 egg, beaten
1½ c. raw cranberries, halved
¾ c. chopped walnuts

DIRECTIONS Sift together dry ingredients into large bowl. To the juice of the orange, add oil and enough boiling water to make ¾ c.; stir into dry ingredients. Add beaten egg and zest. Stir in cranberries and nuts. Bake in greased bread pan for one hour. Cool, wrap in plastic wrap, and store in refrigerator 24 hours before slicing. May be frozen for later use.

1 Trim patterned paper to fit around bread; affix sticker.
2 Stamp fresh baked and house on sticker. 3 Create text box in software; change color to tan. Type "We're thankful for you". Print on cardstock and punch out. Attach to metal-rim tag; attach eyelet. 4 Tie tag around bread with jute.

SUPPLIES: *Cardstock:* (white) *Patterned paper:* (Taylor) Melissa Frances *Clear stamps:* (fresh baked, house from Holiday Treats set) Papertrey Inc. *Dye ink:* (Vermillion Lacquer) Ranger Industries *Pigment ink:* (Vintage Sepia) Tsukineko *Accents:* (metal-rim tag) Making Memories; (silver eyelet) *Sticker:* (date label) Melissa Frances *Fibers:* (jute) Making Memories *Font:* (Cluffhmk) www.fonts101.com *Software:* (word processing) Microsoft *Tools:* (1⅜" circle punch) EK Success; (tag maker) Making Memories **Finished size: 10¾" x 5½"**

SUPPLIES: *Cardstock:* (Ruby Red, Always Artichoke, Chocolate Chip, Natural Ivory) Stampin' Up! *Patterned paper:* (Red Antique Floral from Ancestry.com collection) K&Company *Rubber stamps:* (please come, enjoy from Fancy Flexible Phrases set) Stampin' Up! *Dye ink:* (Close to Cocoa, Always Artichoke) Stampin' Up! *Accents:* (paper-wrapped wire stems, staple, antique bronze photo corners) *Fibers:* (cranberry ruffle ribbon) Making Memories; (white floss) *Font:* (Selfish) www.dafont.com *Adhesive:* (foam tape) *Tool:* (decorative-edge scissors) *Other:* (silk rose, tea bag) **Finished sizes: invitation 5½" x 4¼"; favor 2½" x 3"; roses 5½" diameter x 12½" height**

⁙5⁙ Tea & Roses Party Designer: Jessica Witty

INVITATION ❶ Make card from cardstock. ❷ Trim patterned paper slightly smaller than card front; ink edges and adhere. ❸ Stamp please come on cardstock. Trim, ink edges, and mat with cardstock; adhere. ❹ Tie ribbon around card. Attach photo corners. ❺ Print sentiment on cardstock. Trim and ink edges; mat with cardstock and adhere with foam tape.

FAVOR ❶ Make pocket from cardstock. ❷ Cut strip of patterned paper; ink edges. Adhere ribbon; adhere to pocket. ❸ Ink floss and adhere to tea bag. ❹ Stamp enjoy on card-stock. Trim and ink edges; staple to floss. ❺ Insert tea bag in pocket.

ROSE ❶ Remove petals and leaves from head of silk rose. Keep remaining cone and stem holder. ❷ Cut petals and leaves, following patterns on p. 175. Ink petals. ❸ Pull petals over bone folder or table edge to soften and separate cardstock layers. Peel petals apart. ❹ Curl petals slightly. Adhere, smallest to largest, to silk rose cone. ❺ Trim leaves with decorative-edge scissors. Trace veins with embossing stylus; ink edges. Pull over bone folder or table edge to soften. ❻ Curl and adhere leaves to rose and stem.

DESIGNER TIP

When forming roses, adhere each petal peeking from behind the two in front of it. Work and fold petals as you go so the rose takes on a natural shape.

Buttermilk Scones Ana Cabrera

Making the move from California to Utah was not an easy one. My girls and I have always been Cali girls, after all. When we first arrived here, one thing that we fell in love with was the fried scones at a local eatery. This new, yet simple thing—little bits of fried dough—was a small comfort that made our transition a little easier.

INGREDIENTS

2 c. buttermilk (warmed to 115 degrees)
1 pkg. yeast
1 tbsp. sugar
3 tbsp. oil
2 eggs
½ tsp. salt
½ tsp. baking soda
2 tsp. baking powder
4 c. flour, plus more for dusting

DIRECTIONS Mix together liquids and yeast until yeast dissolves. Mix in flour, one cup at a time. Dough will be fairly sticky. Turn out onto floured surface, and very lightly knead in ½ c. flour until dough is no longer sticky, but still very soft. Place dough ball in large bowl. Let rise for 1 hour. Transfer to fridge for at least 2 hours.

Heat shortening or vegetable oil in pan to 350 degrees. Working with small sections at a time, roll dough out to ½" thick, cut into rectangles (approx. 3" x 4"), and fry in oil. Flip over once, remove when golden brown. Serve with honey butter or sprinkled with powdered sugar.

SUPPLIES: All supplies from Making Memories unless otherwise noted. *Cardstock:* (kraft) Bazzill Basics Paper *Patterned paper:* (Abby Words, Emery Stripe, Emery Dots, Emery Red from Cheeky collection) *Specialty paper:* (photo) Epson *Accents:* (assorted flowers; clear, pink rhinestone brads; epoxy brads; chipboard letters) *Stickers:* (kraft polka dot tape) *Font:* (CK Invitation) Creating Keepsakes; (Rickles) www.dafont.com; (Futura) www.fonts.com *Software:* (photo editing) Adobe *Other:* (lunchbox, white floral wire, floral foam, bamboo picks, digital photo) no source **Finished sizes: invitation 6" x 4½", centerpiece 7¾" x 12" x 6", food picks 1½" x 4"**

Tween Slumber Party
Designer: Ana Cabrera

INVITATION ❶ Make card from cardstock. Adhere patterned paper strip. ❷ Create 5½" x 4" project in software. Fill with hot pink. Drop in photo and type invitation text. ❸ Print on photo paper; trim and adhere. ❹ Affix tape.

CENTERPIECE ❶ Fill lunchbox with floral foam. ❷ Cut shapes of pajama top, bottoms, and slippers from two layers of patterned paper. Stitch pieces together, leaving section open at bottom. ❸ Curve end of wire piece into hook. Slide into pajama pieces and adhere. ❹ Mat chipboard letter with patterned paper. Cut patterned paper to fit behind mat and adhere wire hook between layers. ❺ Arrange wired shapes in floral foam. ❻ Attach brads to flowers; press into foam.

FOOD PICKS Adhere chipboard letters to picks.

ACCENT ❶ Die-cut bee from patterned paper. Ink edges of wings and body. ❷ Cut off antennae; adhere knotted twine. ❸ Cut cardstock strips; ink edges and adhere. Draw face with marker. ❹ Stitch wings with floss. Adhere twine loops. Adhere wings to body.

CARD ❶ Make card from cardstock. ❷ Cut slightly smaller patterned paper piece; ink edges and adhere. ❸ Stamp "Honey!" on cardstock. Apply rub-on. Trim, ink edges, and mat with fabric scrap. Trim edges with decorative-edge scissors; stitch edges. ❹ Mat piece with patterned paper; ink edges and adhere. ❺ Adhere accent with foam tape.

Bonus Idea

This card is a cute play on the honey that you would put on the scones.

SUPPLIES: *Cardstock:* (Warm White) Prism; (Kraft) DMD, Inc. *Patterned paper:* (Gracie, Abby, Bernice) Melissa Frances *Clear stamps:* (Lowercase Circa alphabet) Provo Craft *Chalk ink:* (Bisque, Chestnut Roan) Clearsnap *Color medium:* (black marker) *Accent:* (gold floral fabric scrap) *Rub-on:* (sentiment) Melissa Frances *Fibers:* (hemp twine) Stampin' Up!; (blue floss) *Adhesive:* (foam tape) *Die:* (bee) Provo Craft *Tools:* (die cut machine) Provo Craft; (decorative-edge scissors) **Finished size: 4½" x 5½"**

Best Ever Rolls Nancy Davies

We have a family friend who makes wonderful bread and rolls. He taught me his secrets to making perfect bread, and when he moved across the country a few years ago, I carried on the tradition of fresh homemade rolls. I developed this recipe myself, and it is my most requested creation.

INGREDIENTS

1½ c. milk
½ c. water
¼ c. butter
5–5½ c. flour
½ c. sugar
2 tsp. salt
1 tbsp. quick-rise yeast
1 egg, well-beaten

DIRECTIONS Heat milk, water, and butter until butter is melted and liquid is very warm (120 to 130 degrees). While liquid heats, combine 4 c. flour, sugar, salt, and yeast. Add liquid to dry mixture; add one egg. Mix well. Work in remaining flour as needed, a little at a time until dough is no longer sticky. Knead until smooth and elastic, about 5 minutes. Shape into smooth ball, and place in lightly oiled bowl. Oil top of dough lightly; cover. Let rise about 30 minutes in a warm place.

Punch down dough and divide into 4 balls; cover again and let rest 10 minutes. Form into rolls and place on greased pan, lightly oiling tops. Cover and let rise in a warm place until doubled, about 45 minutes. Bake in preheated oven at 375 degrees until lightly golden, about 15 to 17 minutes. Brush tops with butter after removing from oven to keep them soft.

Best Ever Hostess Tag
Designer: Lindsey Botkin

① Cut tag from patterned paper. ② Print sentiment on cardstock; trim. Trim one edge with decorative-edge scissors; adhere. ③ Adhere patterned paper. Apply swirl rub-on. ④ Apply flower rub-on to patterned paper; trim to fit behind frame and adhere. Adhere to tag. ⑤ Adhere trim. Cover chipboard flower with patterned paper, tie with ribbon, and adhere. Insert pin. ⑥ Punch circle from patterned paper; cut in half and adhere to tag. Punch hole and tie with ribbon.

DESIGNER TIP

Make your favorite hostess' day with a basket of rolls and a tag to let her know how much you appreciated her hospitality.

SUPPLIES: *Cardstock:* (Whisper White) Stampin' Up! *Patterned paper:* (peach, aqua, green floral from Little Girls pack) Cosmo Cricket *Accents:* (white frame) Melissa Frances: (chipboard flower) Stampin' Up!; (beaded stick pin) Making Memories *Rub-ons:* (swirl, flower) Me & My Big Ideas *Fibers:* (white polka dot sheer ribbon) May Arts; (white crocheted trim) Melissa Frances *Font:* (your choice) *Tools:* (1" circle punch, decorative-edge scissors) **Finished size: 3½" x 6¼"**

Potluck Picks   Designer: Kim Hughes

① Print food names on cardstock. ② Punch hearts from card-stock; adhere over printed text. Print text again. ③ Punch circles from printed cardstock. ④ Punch eight circles from cardstock for each pick. Adhere behind printed circle, forming scalloped edge. ⑤ Adhere toothpick to back of piece. Punch circle from cardstock; adhere to back of piece. ⑥ Tie ribbon.

SUPPLIES: *Cardstock:* (brown, ivory, pink) Bazzill Basics Paper *Fibers:* (pink grosgrain ribbon) Beaux Regards *Fonts:* (French Script) www.myfonts.com; (Teletype) www.simplythebest.net *Tools:* (1¼", ½" circle, heart punches) EK Success *Other:* (toothpicks) **Finished size: 1¾" x 3¾"**

Cheesy Garlic Drop Biscuits Alisa Bangerter

This is a perfect recipe if you are short on time because there is no rolling or cutting. The cheese and garlic add extra kick to a plain biscuit. They are perfect to serve with soups or stews, and are great served with a salad.

INGREDIENTS

2 c. flour
2 tbsp. granulated sugar
4 tsp. baking powder
1½ tsp. garlic powder
½ tsp. salt
⅔ c. butter or margarine
1½ c. grated cheddar cheese
1¼ c. milk
Chives (optional)

DIRECTIONS Mix together dry ingredients. Cut in butter with pastry cutter until mixture is fine. Add cheese and mix well. Add milk and stir until just moistened. Drop by spoonfuls onto greased baking sheet. Sprinkle top with chives if desired. Bake at 400 degrees for approx. 15 minutes.

SUPPLIES: *Cardstock:* (Peanut) Bazzill Basics Paper; (white) *Patterned paper:* (BBQ Checks from BBQ collection) Pebbles Inc. *Dye ink:* (Coffee Bean) Paper Salon *Accents:* (yellow buttons) American Crafts; (white flowers) Making Memories *Fibers:* (red gingham ribbon) Offray; (yellow polka dot ribbon) Michaels; (yellow floss) DMC *Font:* (Minya Nouvelle) www.dafont.com *Other:* (wood skewers, green floral wire, paper cord) **Finished sizes: invitation 5¼" x 7½", food picks 1¾" x 7¾", napkin ring 8" x 1½"**

⑤ Summer Picnic Party Designer: Wendy Johnson

INVITATION ❶ Print invitation on cardstock; fold. Cut into basket. ❷ Cut cardstock to fit card front. Cut ½" cardstock strips; ink edges. Weave and adhere to block. Trim edges. ❸ Cut patterned paper; ink edges. Fold over block; adhere. Curl edges up. ❹ Adhere paper cord to card front. Thread buttons with floss; adhere to flowers. Adhere wire to flowers. Adhere flowers to cord and card front. ❺ Adhere block to card front. ❻ Print "Let's picnic!" on cardstock. Trim into tag, punch hole, and tie to cord with ribbon.

FOOD PICKS

❶ Thread buttons with floss; adhere to flowers. ❷ Adhere flowers to skewers. ❸ Print food text on cardstock. Trim into tag, punch hole, and tie to skewer with ribbon.

NAPKIN RING

❶ Cut ribbon to finished length; notch end. Adhere end to form ring. ❷ Thread button with floss; adhere to flower. Adhere flower to ring.

Danish Aebleskivers Susan Neal

This recipe was introduced to me shortly after I moved to Utah. I quickly bought the pans to make it. It is one of the yummiest things I have ever eaten, and so darn cute!

AEBLESKIVERS INGREDIENTS

2 c. buttermilk
2 eggs, separated
2 c. flour
1 tsp. soda
1 tsp. baking powder
½ tsp. salt
2 tsp. sugar

DIRECTIONS Sift together flour, baking soda, and baking powder. Beat egg yolks in large bowl. Add sugar, salt, milk, and sifted mixture. Fold in stiffly beaten egg whites. Place in aebleskiver pan and cook approx. 5 minutes, turning once, until brown and cooked through.

BUTTERSCOTCH SYRUP INGREDIENTS

1½ c. sugar
1½ cubes butter
2 tbsp. white corn syrup
¾ c. buttermilk
1 tsp. soda
2 tsp. vanilla

DIRECTIONS Combine all ingredients but vanilla in saucepan. Cook 7 minutes, stirring every so often, barely boiling. Remove from heat and add vanilla.

VARIATION: SPRINKLE SLICED ALMONDS ON TOP.

5 STEPS Vintage Game Night Party

Designer: Susan Neal

INVITATION ❶ Make card from cardstock. Cover with patterned paper; sand edges. ❷ Cut cardstock strip; mat with cardstock, attach stars, and adhere. ❸ Print tag frame and "Vintage game board night" on cardstock; trim and adhere with foam tape. *Note: Frame is a character in CBX Tags font.* ❹ Print party details on cardstock; trim. Mat with cardstock, attach star, and adhere inside card.

CLIPBOARD ❶ Cover clipboard with patterned paper; sand edges. ❷ Print scoreboard title, frame, and names on cardstock; trim. Draw lines with pencil. ❸ Double-mat with cardstock, attach star, and attach under clip. ❹ Tie pencil to clip with jute.

RECIPE TAGS ❶ Print recipe on cardstock; trim into tags. Cut tag from patterned paper; sand edges. ❷ Mat all tags with cardstock; punch hole. ❸ Tie tags together with jute. Attach star to top tag.

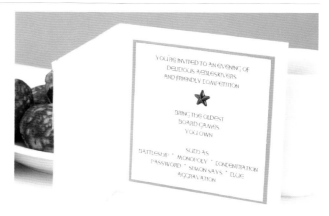

Inside

SUPPLIES: *Cardstock:* (Petunia, Parakeet, Bitter Chocolate, white) Bazzill Basics Paper *Patterned paper:* (vintage icons from Urban Rhapsody collection) K&Company *Accents:* (metal star studs) Scrapworks *Fibers:* (brown jute) *Fonts:* (CBX Tags) Chatterbox; (LD Roman Engraving) www.letteringdelights.com *Adhesive:* (foam tape) *Tool:* (⅛" circle punch) *Other:* (small clipboard) Wal-Mart; (pencil) **Finished sizes: invitation 5" square, clipboard 6" x 9", recipe tags 2¾" x 4¾"**

Christmas Breakfast Stocking

Designer: Kim Kesti

1 Cut pocket pieces, following pattern on p. 175. Adhere pieces together. *Note: Adhere pocket only on three sides.* 2 Punch eight circles from patterned paper; ink edges and adhere. *Note: Trim circles to match pocket edge.* 3 Adhere trim and rickrack. Stitch and ink edges. 4 Punch hole and tie with ribbon. 5 Cut tag from cardstock with decorative-edge scissors; punch hole. Spell name with stickers; attach to pocket with safety pin. Insert candy cane.

SUPPLIES: *Cardstock:* (Vanilla, In the Pink Shimmer) Bazzill Basics Paper *Patterned paper:* (Lulubelle from Pink Lemonade collection) Webster's Pages; (Ava Artisan Edge Die Cut from Noteworthy collection) Making Memories *Accent:* (cream safety pin) Making Memories *Stickers:* (Newsprint alphabet) Heidi Swapp *Fibers:* (cream ribbon) Offray; (white flower trim, pink rickrack) *Tools:* (decorative-edge scissors) Fiskars; (1", ⅛" circle punches) *Other:* (candy cane) **Finished size: 5¼" x 7¾"**

Twisty Pretzels
Brenda Peterson

These pretzels are ideal for cooking with kids. I made this recipe with my daycare kids and we would have a blast! They loved creating unique designs like the letters in their name or geometric shapes.

INGREDIENTS

1⅓ c. water (110 degrees)
2½ tbsp. butter
1½ tbsp. sugar
1 tsp. salt
4 c. flour
2½ tsp. quick-rise yeast
5 tsp. baking soda
Kosher salt (optional)

DIRECTIONS Dissolve sugar and yeast in warm water. Let set 5 minutes. Mix in butter, flour, and salt. Roll out dough in a rounded rectangle and cut into strips. Shape strips into pretzels. Cover and let rise for 45 minutes.

In non-aluminum pan, add 2" water and soda; bring to boil. Boil pretzels 1 minute, turning once. Place on greased baking sheet. Brush with melted butter and sprinkle with salt. Bake at 450 degrees for 10 to 12 minutes.

SUPPLIES: *Cardstock:* (green, blue, black, white) *Accents:* (black brads) *Stickers:* (Pajamas alphabet) American Crafts; (comma) Scenic Route *Font:* (Century Gothic) Microsoft *Other:* (wood dowel) Oriental Trading Co. **Finished sizes: invitation 4¾" x 6", coaster 7" x 5", drink flag 9" x 13"**

:5: Monday Night Football Party Designer: Teri Anderson

INVITATION ❶ Cut cardstock to finished size. Print invitation on cardstock; trim and adhere. ❷ Adhere cardstock strip; attach brads. ❸ Print "Go team" on cardstock; trim into flag shape. Mat with cardstock and adhere. ❹ Attach brads to cardstock strips; adhere.

COASTER ❶ Cut triangle from cardstock; double-mat with cardstock. ❷ Cut cardstock strips; adhere. Attach brads. ❸ Affix stickers.

DRINK FLAG ❶ Cut triangle from cardstock; double-mat with cardstock. ❷ Print "Another cold one!" on cardstock; trim and adhere. ❸ Affix stickers. ❹ Cut rectangles from cardstock. Fold over dowel; adhere to flag. *Note: Flag should be able to slide along dowel.* Attach brads.

DESIGNER TIP

Raise the flag to request another drink.

Thanks Bag Topper

Designer: Valerie Pingree

① Make topper from cardstock. ② Adhere cardstock strip behind scallop holes. ③ Adhere cardstock strips. ④ Spell "Thanks" with stickers. Adhere salt; let dry. ⑤ Punch holes through topper and cellophane bag; tie with ribbon.

SUPPLIES: *Cardstock:* (Lily White, Lemon Lime, Bubblegum, Pajama) Doodlebug Design; (Bazzill White scalloped) Bazzill Basics Paper *Stickers:* (Milan alphabet) American Crafts *Fibers:* (striped ribbon) Strano Designs *Other:* (Epsom salt, cellophane bag) **Finished size: 5¾" x 4"**

Pumpkin Muffins Alisa Bangerter

My favorite time to make these yummy muffins is in the fall. The added spices complement the pumpkin perfectly. You can change the flavor of the muffins by adding nuts, raisins, or chocolate chips. I like to make these muffins using a tiny muffin tin, which makes a nice size for gift giving or for brunch.

INGREDIENTS

1½ c. flour
1 tsp. baking powder
1 tsp. baking soda
¼ tsp. salt
1 tsp. ground cinnamon
1 tsp. ground nutmeg
1 tsp. ground cloves
¾ c. vegetable oil
1 c. granulated sugar
1 c. mashed canned pumpkin
2 eggs
½ c. raisins, nuts, or chocolate chips (optional)

DIRECTIONS Mix together dry ingredients, set aside. In large bowl, combine sugar and oil. Add eggs and mix well. Add dry ingredients to wet mixture and mix well. Add pumpkin and raisins, nuts, or chocolate chips. Bake at 350 degrees for approx. 20 minutes.

INVITATION ❶ Cut cardstock to finished size. ❷ Print invitation on cardstock; trim. Mat with patterned paper, zigzag-stitch seams, and adhere. ❸ Cut patterned paper strip. Punch 10 circles from patterned paper; adhere behind bottom edge of strip to form scallops. Adhere. ❹ Tie ribbon.

FAVOR BAG ❶ Cover front of gift bag with patterned paper. ❷ Adhere patterned paper strip. ❸ Print "No tricks. Just treats!" on cardstock; trim. Mat with cardstock, stitch edges, and adhere. ❹ Punch hearts from patterned paper; adhere. ❺ Wrap ribbon around bag handles; adhere inside bag and knot.

FOOD PICKS ❶ Cut ghost and skull shapes, following pattern on p. 175. Punch out eyes. ❷ Punch circle from cardstock; mat with punched patterned paper circle. Adhere shape. ❸ Adhere craft stick to back of piece. Punch circle from cardstock; adhere over craft stick. ❹ Tie with ribbon.

SUPPLIES: *Cardstock:* (black, white) *Patterned paper:* (Flocked Spider from Halloween collection) Making Memories; (Flower Sprig-Lace from Hollie's collection) Scribble Scrabble; (Baby Girl Dots from Baby Girl collection) Heidi Grace Designs *Fibers:* (pale yellow swirl ribbon) Creative Impressions *Font:* (Tootlebug) www.searchfreefonts.com *Tools:* (⅛", ½", 1½", 1¾" circle punches, heart punch) EK Success *Other:* (white gift bag, craft sticks) **Finished sizes: invitation 5" square, favor bag 4" x 5¼", food picks 1¾" x 3¾"**

SUPPLIES: *Cardstock:* (white) *Patterned paper:* (Hocus Pocus) Doodlebug Design; (purple flourish) *Color medium:* (black marker) *Accents:* (skull, purple, black, white, orange epoxy brads) Making Memories; (silver brad) *Stickers:* (Hopscotch alphabet) Doodlebug Design; (purple photo corners) American Crafts *Fibers:* (orange striped ribbon) Making Memories; (purple twill ribbon) *Font:* (Agency) www.fonts.com *Adhesive:* (repositionable) *Other:* (cupcake box) Wilton Enterprises; (chipboard) **Finished size: 6¼" x 3" x 6¼"**

5 STEPS Spooking Box Designer: Brandy Jesperson

BOX ❶ Cover box sides with patterned paper. ❷ Cut cardstock slightly smaller than box top. Draw ghost using marker. Spell "Boo" with stickers. ❸ Mat piece with patterned paper; adhere to box top with repositionable adhesive.

SWIVEL PANEL ❶ Cut patterned paper to fit box top. Cut swirl with craft knife and attach epoxy brads. ❷ Print text on cardstock; trim. Adhere under swirl. Affix photo corners. ❸ Adhere piece to chipboard. ❹ Cut prongs from skull brad; adhere to silver brad. ❺ Attach ribbon and panel to box with brad.

Open

Apple Muffins Alisa Bangerter

I love to make these muffins for breakfast or for lunch. They are really moist and the apple adds extra nutrition. If I want the muffins to be chunkier, I chop the apples instead of grate them.

APPLE MUFFIN INGREDIENTS

1 egg
½ c. milk
¼ c. vegetable oil
1 c. grated raw tart apple (unpared)
1½ c. flour
⅓ c. sugar
2¼ tsp. baking powder
½ tsp. salt
½ tsp. cinnamon
¼ tsp. nutmeg

DIRECTIONS Slightly beat egg. Stir in milk, oil, and apple. Mix together dry ingredients. Stir in dry ingredients to wet mixture until moistened. Fill greased muffin cups ⅔ full with batter and sprinkle tops with topping mixture. Bake at 400 degrees for 20 to 25 minutes or until done.

TOPPING INGREDIENTS

⅓ c. brown sugar
⅓ c. chopped nuts
½ tsp. cinnamon

DIRECTIONS Mix ingredients together and sprinkle over top of batter in each muffin cup.

SUPPLIES: *Cardstock:* (brown, tan, blue, white) *Patterned paper:* (polka dot, multi stripe, blue stripe from Funky pad) KI Memories *Accents:* (Capitol Hill chipboard alphabet) Scenic Route *Stickers:* (Center of Attention alphabet) Heidi Swapp; (Whistle Stop alphabet) American Crafts; (tab, labels, heart, cool, stars, squares, circles, border) KI Memories; (September, journaling circle, square) Reminisce; (brown, white alphabet) *Die:* (scalloped circle) Spellbinders *Tools:* (die cut machine) Spellbinders; (corner rounder punch) Marvy Uchida *Other:* (pencils) **Finished sizes: card 5½" square, food picks large 4¾" x 7½", medium 4¼" x 7½", round 3½" x 7½"**

Back to School Breakfast Ensemble
Designer: Nicole Keller

CARD ❶ Make card from cardstock. Cover with patterned paper; round bottom corners. ❷ Adhere patterned paper strips. ❸ Embellish with stickers and chipboard. Adhere pencil.

FOOD PICKS ❶ Cut rectangles from cardstock. Die-cut scalloped circle from cardstock. ❷ Cover rectangles with patterned paper; round corners of large piece. ❸ Embellish with stickers and chipboard. ❹ Adhere pieces to pencils.

SUPPLIES: *Patterned paper:* (Conversation, Linen from Brunch collection) Crate Paper *Clear stamps:* (label, sentiment circle from Holiday Treats set) Papertrey Ink *Dye ink:* (brown) Stampin' Up! *Accents:* (chipboard apples) American Crafts; (yellow button) Autumn Leaves; (brown brads) Making Memories; (green bar brad) Karen Foster Design *Fibers:* (red rickrack) Crate Paper; (red floss, jute) *Dies:* (frame, scalloped square) *Tool:* (die cut machine) Provo Craft *Other:* (paper bag) **Finished size: 6" x 9½"**

Fresh-Baked Treats Gift Bag   Designer: Betsy Veldman

❶ Die-cut frame and scalloped square from patterned paper; sand edges, layer, and adhere together. Stitch square edges. ❷ Stamp label on patterned paper; trim and adhere to piece. Attach brads. Adhere chipboard apple. ❸ Sand edges of chipboard apple; adhere. Stamp sentiment circle on patterned paper; trim and adhere. Thread button with floss and adhere. ❹ Adhere piece to bag. Fold bag top down. ❺ Punch holes in bag top. Tie rickrack and jute to bar brad; attach. ❻ Cut tab from patterned paper; adhere over bag top.

What's not to love about desserts? After all, whether they're eaten as part of a meal or as a special stand-alone treat, they're always delicious. And, not only are these scrumptious paper-crafted projects calorie free, they're sure to make eating these desserts even more enjoyable. So, go on, dig in to these tasty delights and start celebrating the joy of living.

DESSERTS

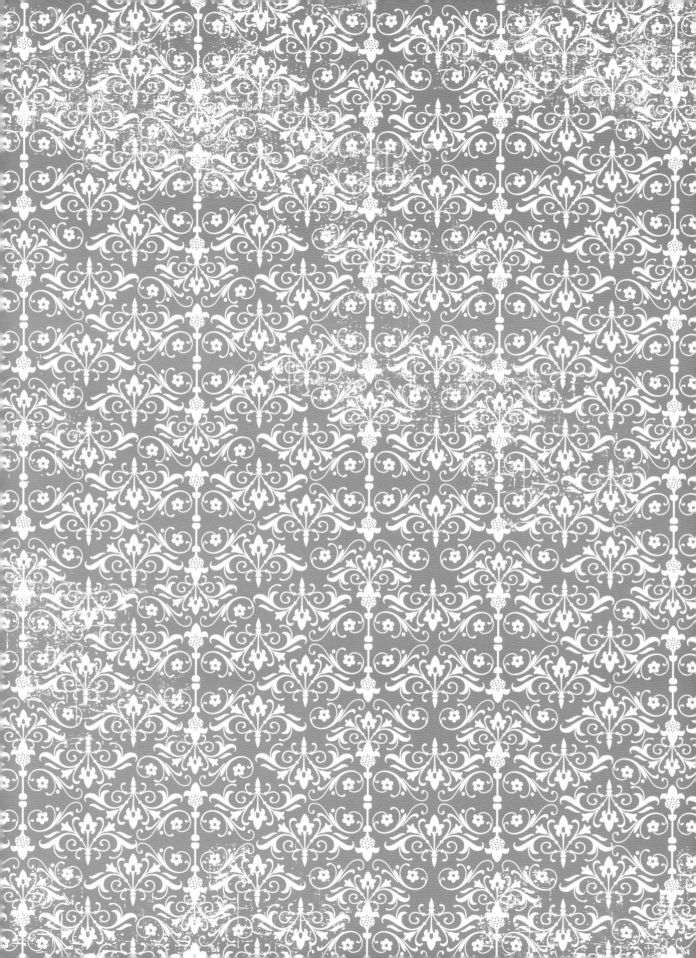

Yummy Sandwich Cookies Brenda Peterson

can't eat just one. My daughter and I love to make these cookies, which is so easy to do. Plus, these cookies are great for pot lucks and bake sales!

COOKIE INGREDIENTS

2 pkgs. Devil's Food cake mix
1 c. vegetable oil
4 large eggs

ICING INGREDIENTS

½ c. margarine
1 pkg. (8 oz.) cream cheese
2 tsp. vanilla
3-4 c. icing sugar

DIRECTIONS Mix cookie ingredients together. Roll mix into small balls and place on cookie sheet. Bake 10 to 12 minutes at 350 degrees. Cool until chilled.

For icing: Combine ingredients.

Assemble: Cover each cookie with icing and place another cookie on top of it to make the cookie sandwich. Chill until cookies are firm.

SUPPLIES: *Cardstock:* (white) WorldWin *Patterned paper:* (Confetti, Cake & Ice Cream, Clown Nose, Surprise, Kazoo Blue, Frosting from Cupcake collection) BasicGrey *Color medium:* (black pen) EK Success *Accents:* (star brads) Oriental Trading Co.; (star eyelet) The Eyelet Factory *Stickers:* (Cupcake alphabet, scalloped border, swirls) BasicGrey *Fibers:* (red twill ribbon) Offray *Tools:* (corner rounder punch) McGill; (2¼" square punch, decorative-edge scissors) *Other:* (red gift bag) Wal-Mart; (wood spoon) **Finished sizes: invitation 6" x 5½", memory game cards 2½" square, game bag 5¼" x 8½", game spoon tag 5" x 1¾"**

5 STEPS · Circus Party
Designer: Nicole Keller

INVITATION ❶ Make invitation from cardstock, following pattern on p. 176. ❷ Cut patterned paper pieces for tent top and middle, using invitation as guide. Ink edges and adhere. ❸ Cut strip of patterned paper, using invitation as guide. Trim one edge using decorative-edge scissors. Ink edges with pen and adhere. ❹ Affix stickers and attach brads. ❺ Spell "Circus fun!" with stickers.

MEMORY GAME CARDS ❶ Adhere patterned paper to front and back of cardstock. Punch squares for game cards; round corners. ❷ Cut cupcake, ice cream, and popsicle images from patterned paper; adhere to cards. ❸ Tie cards together with ribbon. ❹ Attach brads.

GAME BAG *Ink all edges with pen.* ❶ Remove bag handles. ❷ Affix stickers to bag. ❸ Affix alphabet stickers to patterned paper to spell "Team". Trim and mat with patterned paper. Round corners and adhere. ❹ Affix 2 to patterned paper. Trim and mat with patterned paper. Trim using decorative-edge

scissors. Mat piece with patterned paper. Round corners and adhere. ❺ Attach brad to bag.

GAME SPOON ❶ Make tag from patterned paper. Round corners and ink edges with pen. ❷ Spell "Team 1" with stickers on patterned paper. Trim, mat with patterned paper, round edges, and adhere to tag. ❸ Set eyelet. ❹ Tie ribbon to tag and wood spoon. ❺ Attach brad.

BONUS IDEA

Use the gift bag and game piece to play a popcorn relay race. Simply divide all the kids at the party into two teams. Place two bowls of popcorn 20 feet from the paper bags, and have the kids compete to see which team can run and scoop up the popcorn with the wood spoons and empty the most popcorn into the paper bags before the time runs out. *Note: To maximize the fun and make the game a true relay race, be sure to have team members take turns scooping up the popcorn and emptying it into the bags.*

TREAT CAN ❶ Cut 2½" x 6" window in container using craft knife. Cover container and lid with patterned paper. *Note: Cut window from patterned paper to match container window.* ❷ Adhere transparency piece behind window. ❸ Adhere cardstock strips. ❹ Attach brads and adhere ribbon.

TAG ❶ Make tag from cardstock. ❷ Affix sticker and apply rub-on. ❸ Punch circle from patterned paper; adhere to tag. Punch hole. ❹ Tie on ribbon.

SUPPLIES: *Cardstock:* (lime green) Die Cuts With a View *Patterned paper:* (Roxie Bands from Love, Elsie collection) KI Memories *Transparency sheet:* Hammermill *Accents:* (black brads) Doodlebug Design *Rub-on:* (sentiment) American Crafts *Sticker:* (piano) EK Success *Fibers:* (lime green grosgrain ribbon) *Tool:* (¾" circle punch) *Other:* (potato chip container) **Finished sizes: treat can 3" diameter x 9¾" height, tag 2¾" x 5"**

Coconut Croissant Pudding Susan Neal

This is one of those "necessity is the mother of invention" recipes. I was having some family over for dinner and needed a quick, easy dessert. I saw my two-day-old croissants and instantly thought about making an easy bread pudding with two of my favorite ingredients: coconut and dulce de leche*.

INGREDIENTS

5 two-day-old croissants
1 pkg. instant vanilla (or coconut) pudding, prepared
1 jar dulce de leche
¼ c. hot milk
¼ c. toasted coconut
Whipped cream

DIRECTIONS Tear croissants into small pieces. Layer croissant pieces and pudding in 10 individual 6 oz. (3.5") ramekins. Wisk hot milk into warmed dulce de leche until it can be poured. Pour dulce de leche over the top, letting it ooze down in between the layers. Sprinkle with toasted coconut. Dollop whipped cream and sprinkle with the rest of the coconut.

DON'T HAVE ANY DULCE DE LECHE ON HAND? MAKE SOME WITH CONDENSED MILK AND YOUR MICROWAVE!

Microwave Dulce de Leche: Pour 1 can condensed milk into a 2 quart glass measuring cup.

Cook on 50% power for 4 minutes (stir every 2 minutes until smooth).

Cook on 30% power for 20 to 25 minutes, or until thick and caramel colored.

Stir every 4 minutes for the first 15 minutes, then every 2 minutes during the last 6 to 10 minutes of cooking.

INVITATION ❶ Make card from transparency sheet. Stamp Floral Background on card front. ❷ Cut two squares of cardstock slightly smaller than card front. Adhere inside card. ❸ Stamp you're invited on cardstock. Trim and adhere. ❹ Tie ribbon around card front and adhere.

CANDLEHOLDER ❶ Cut transparency to fit candleholder. ❷ Stamp Floral Background; adhere to candleholder. ❸ Tie ribbon.

FAVOR BOX ❶ Stamp Floral Background on box. ❷ Fill box with candy; tie ribbon. ❸ Stamp enjoy! on cardstock. Trim and adhere.

SUPPLIES: *Cardstock:* (Gunmetal) The Paper Studio *Transparency sheet:* Office Depot *Rubber stamps:* (Floral Background) Stampin' Up!; (you're invited, enjoy! from Wedding Essentials set) Paper Salon *Pigment ink:* (Graphite Black) Tsukineko *Solvent ink:* (Cotton White) Tsukineko *Fibers:* (black ribbon) Offray *Other:* (glass candleholder) Michaels; (acrylic pillow box) Inky Antics; (candy) **Finished sizes: invitation 4¼" square, candleholder 3½" diameter x 4" height, favor box 4" x 6" x 1¼"**

SUPPLIES: All supplies from Melissa Frances unless otherwise noted. *Cardstock:* (Blossom) Bazzill Basics Paper *Patterned paper:* (Thankful from Thankful collection, Paige from Ambiente collection, Cecilia from This Moment on Wedding collection) *Clear stamp:* (frame from Frame Work set) *Dye ink:* (Old Paper) Ranger Industries *Chalk ink:* (Rose Coral) Clearsnap *Accents:* (white keyhole); (pink glitter brads) Doodlebug Design; (cream flowers) no source *Rub-ons:* (sentiment) *Sticker:* (wedding trousseau) *Fibers:* (white lace trim) *Tools:* (decorative-edge scissors) no source **Finished size: 4½" x 6"**

Bridal Shower Invitation Designer: Melissa Phillips

CARD BASE

❶ Make card from cardstock. ❷ Cut patterned paper to fit card front. Trim with decorative-edge scissors and ink edges. Pierce along sides.

ACCENT PIECE

❶ Cut patterned paper smaller than card front. Ink edges.
❷ Cut tag shape from patterned paper. Stamp frame, ink edges, and adhere. ❸ Apply rub-on. Ink edges of sticker; affix. Adhere keyhole. ❹ Adhere lace trim. ❺ Attach brads to flowers and adhere piece to card base.

Raspberry Cream Cheese Coffee Cake Nicole Keller

originally got the idea for this recipe from a message board on the internet. Although it was very good, I thought it could be perfected. I played with the recipe and came up with the topping. That seemed to give it the finishing touch it needed, and is what induces the raves from everyone when I make it.

COFFEE CAKE INGREDIENTS

1 pkg. (8 oz.) cream cheese, softened
1 c. granulated sugar
½ c. butter, softened
1¾ c. flour
2 eggs
¼ c. milk
1 tsp. vanilla
1 tsp. baking powder
½ tsp. baking soda
¼ tsp. salt
½ c. fruit preserves (raspberry, apricot, or a fruit of your choice)

TOPPING INGREDIENTS

4 oz. cream cheese
¼ c. butter
¼ c. powdered sugar

DIRECTIONS Preheat oven to 350 degrees. Grease and flour a 13" x 9" x 2" pan. In a large bowl, beat cream cheese, granulated sugar, and butter with a mixer until fluffy. Add one cup of flour, eggs, milk, vanilla, baking powder, baking soda, and salt. Beat for 2 minutes until light and fluffy. Beat in remaining flour until well mixed. Spread batter evenly in pan using rubber spatula. *Note: Batter will seem thick.* Spoon preserves over top in 12 to 15 portions. Using a knife, swirl preserves into batter (using back-and-forth, left-to-right, and up-and-down pattern).

Beat topping ingredients together until fluffy. With a spoon, dollop on top of batter in 12 to 15 portions. Bake for 30 to 35 minutes until lightly browned and a toothpick comes out clean. Cool slightly, and sift powdered sugar on top. Serve warm.

SUPPLIES: *Patterned paper:* (Hot Chicks, Drapin' Daisies, Spring Fling, Pretty New Dress, Tiptoe Through Tulips from For Peep's Sake collection) Imaginisce *Accents:* (glitter frame, chick circle, bunny circle die cuts; flower brads, metal tag rims, chipboard flower) Making Memories *Stickers:* (Garden Party alphabet) Making Memories *Fibers:* (green/brown gingham, blue/white polka dot, blue striped, blue grosgrain ribbon) Making Memories; (green gingham, blue grosgrain, blue loop-edge ribbon) American Crafts *Adhesive:* (decoupage) Plaid; (foam tape) *Tools:* (tag, slot punches; tag maker) Making Memories *Other:* (flower pot, chipboard, craft sticks, floral foam, green gift shred, photos) **Finished sizes: invitation 5½" x 5", centerpiece 4½" diameter x 9" height, basket tags 3" x 4½"**

Easter Egg Hunt Party
Designer: Wendy Sue Anderson

INVITATION ❶ Make 11" x 5" card from cardstock. Score at 4¼" from left side and 1¼" from right side. Fold. ❷ Cut square of patterned paper; adhere. ❸ Adhere frame die cut using foam tape. ❹ Knot ribbon and adhere. ❺ Spell "Join us" with stickers.

CENTERPIECE

Flower Pot ❶ Adhere ribbon to flower pot. Tie bow; adhere. ❷ Adhere frame die cut. ❸ Insert floral foam in pot.

Eggs ❶ Cut chipboard flower into five pieces to make eggs. ❷ Cover pieces with patterned paper; sand edges. ❸ Adhere craft sticks to backs.

Assemble Insert eggs in floral foam and add gift shred as desired.

BASKET TAGS ❶ Punch tag from patterned paper. Punch slot. ❷ Adhere circle die cut. Insert photo in metal tag rim; adhere with foam tape. ❸ Attach flower brad and affix stickers to spell child's name. ❹ Tie ribbon. ❺ Repeat steps to make additional tags.

INVITATION ❶ Make card from cardstock. Cover with patterned paper. ❷ Affix banner sticker. ❸ Cut cardstock strip; sand edges. Mat with cardstock; distress edges. ❹ Attach matted strip to card with brads. ❺ Affix stickers to spell "Celebrate". *Note: Mat the "C" and "A" stickers with cardstock.*

BATON ❶ Cut dowel 7" long. ❷ Bundle strips of metallic foil and red trim together. Adhere to dowel. ❸ Wrap ribbon around dowel. Adhere.

SPARKLER BOX WRAP ❶ Cut strip of cardstock to fit box; distress edges. ❷ Sand edges of slightly smaller piece of cardstock; adhere. ❸ Adhere strip of patterned paper. Adhere piece around box. ❹ Affix sticker. Tie trim around box; adhere. ❺ Adhere metallic foil strips and button.

SUPPLIES: All supplies from Close To My Heart unless otherwise noted. *Cardstock:* (Dutch Blue, Outdoor Denim, Cranberry, Honey) *Patterned paper:* (floral, stripe from Blue Ribbon collection) *Accents:* (blue brads); (red button) www.just4funcrafts.com *Stickers:* (Blue Ribbon alphabet, banner, sentiment) *Fibers:* (red trim); (blue grosgrain ribbon) Offray *Other:* (sparkler box) Great Grizzly; (wood dowel, metallic foil) no source **Finished sizes: invitation 7" x 5", baton 8" height, sparkler box wrap 5" x 4½"**

Coconut Goddess Cake Ana Cabrera

This recipe is an adaptation of English trifle (cake, pudding, cream, and fruit). I wanted to have a cake that featured the tropical flavors that I love from the Philippines, my home country. The challenge was coming up with something easy enough for everyday—and this is it. As for the name, Coconut Goddess is my nickname, so this is my signature cake.

INGREDIENTS

1 pkg. yellow cake mix
1 can crushed pineapple
1 c. sugar
2 small boxes instant French vanilla pudding
1 tub whipped topping
1½ c. shredded coconut

DIRECTIONS

Prepare cake following package directions for 13" x 9" cake. While cake is baking, pour pineapple, including juice, into small saucepan. Add sugar. Heat over medium heat until sugar dissolves completely. Bring to a boil, then immediately remove from heat. When cake is done, remove from oven. Using a fork, poke holes in cake about ½" apart. Slather cake with pineapple and juices. Let cool completely.

Make pudding following directions. Let set up in fridge. Spread coconut onto a baking sheet and toast in oven at 325 degrees. *Note: Be sure to stir the coconut often.* Allow coconut to get a light brown, with some bits still white.

Once the cake is completely cool, spread pudding over pineapple layer. Then, spread whipped topping over the top of the pudding and sprinkle with coconut. Chill for one hour.

INVITATION ① Open 3½" x 7" project in software. Drop in flourishes, draw border. Type sentiments and print on cardstock. Make card from printed piece. ② Cut cardstock to finished size. Adhere slightly smaller patterned paper piece. ③ Adhere ends of felt scroll, butterfly die cut, and flat marbles. Slide card under scroll.

BUCKET ① Adhere patterned paper strips to bucket. ② Adhere felt scrolls and butterfly die cuts. ③ Adhere flat marbles.

WASHCLOTH WRAP ① Insert photo in bracelet. ② Roll towel. Wrap bracelet around towel. ③ Adhere felt scrolls and flat marbles to butterfly die cut. ④ Insert completed butterfly behind bracelet.

SUPPLIES: *Cardstock:* (teal, cream) Die Cuts With a View *Patterned paper:* (Word Fresco from Mira collection) K&Company *Accents:* (red, orange, green, blue, purple, brown, white epoxy flat marbles) The Robin's Nest; (butterfly die cuts) K&Company; (blue felt scrolls) Queen & Co. *Digital elements:* (flourishes from Rhonna Swirls kit) www.twopeasinabucket.com *Fonts:* (Scriptina) www.dafont.com; (Algerian Condensed) www.myfonts.com *Software:* (photo editing) *Other:* (red photo bracelet) Making Memories; (metal bucket, teal washcloth, photo) **Finished sizes: invitation 4" x 9¾", bucket 6¾" diameter x 5¾" height, washcloth wrap 5¾" x 4¾"**

[birthday wishes]

SUPPLIES: *Cardstock:* (white) Frances Meyer *Patterned paper:* (Cream Damask from Antique Cream collection) Creative Imaginations; (Greek Revival from Beacon Hill collection) Daisy D's *Dye ink:* (black) *Accents:* (glitter chipboard flower) Melissa Frances; (light brown flower) Bazzill Basics Paper *Rub-ons:* (black stitches) Doodlebug Design; (sentiment) Scenic Route *Fibers:* (white lace trim) Making Memories **Finished size: 6" x 4"**

:5: Birthday Wishes Card Designer: Daniela Dobson

① Make card from cardstock. ② Cut smaller patterned paper piece; mat with patterned paper, and adhere to card front. Ink edges. ③ Apply rub-ons. ④ Adhere flower and chipboard flower. ⑤ Adhere lace trim.

Peanut Butter Brownie Bars

This recipe is special to me because it's the only original recipe I've come up with by myself. I am not a baker, so the fact that these brownies turned out so well makes me feel good. The first time I made these, I gave some to my Dad and with the first bite he closed his eyes and made a long "Mmm" sound. That is something I will always remember.

INGREDIENTS

1 box Pillsbury peanut butter brownie mix (or substitute a plain brownie mix)
1 pkg. (16.5 oz.) Pillsbury peanut butter cookie dough
½ c. flour
½ c. firmly packed brown sugar
4 tbsp. creamy peanut butter
1 Hershey's candy bar

DIRECTIONS Preheat oven to 325 degrees. Grease bottom and sides of 10" round spring form cake pan. In a large bowl, combine ingredients for brownie mix, following package instructions. Pour half of brownie mixture into cake pan and spread evenly. Hand flatten chunks of cookie dough into an even layer and place on top of brownie mixture in pan. Pour remaining brownie mixture on top and spread evenly.

In a small bowl, combine flour, brown sugar, and melted creamy peanut butter. Mix with a fork until coarse crumbs form. Pour evenly over brownies in pan. Bake at 325 degrees for 35 to 45 minutes, or until toothpick inserted in center comes out somewhat clean. Cool for 30 minutes and remove outer ring of spring form pan. Break up chocolate bar and melt in a bowl in the microwave. Drizzle chocolate over peanut butter crumbs with a spoon. Cut into slices and serve.

SUPPLIES: *Patterned paper:* (Rockin', Chillin', Vivid, Expression from About a Boy collection) Fancy Pants Designs *Rub-on:* (sentiment) QuicKutz *Fibers:* (orange/yellow ribbon) May Arts *Die:* (star) QuicKutz *Tools:* (die cut machine) QuicKutz; (2¼", 2½" circle punches) *Other:* (gift box) **Finished size: 6" x 6" x 4¾"**

⁙5⁙ Thanks Gift Box Designer: Jennifer Miller

❶ Cover box lid and sides with patterned paper. ❷ Punch circles from patterned paper. Layer and adhere together.

Die-cut star and adhere. Apply rub-on. ❸ Punch hole in matted circles, insert ribbon, and tie ribbon around box.

SUPPLIES: *Cardstock:* (brown) Bazzill Basics Paper; (cream) Provo Craft *Patterned paper:* (Bliss Friends Flowers from Bohemia 2 collection) My Mind's Eye *Stickers:* (Center of Attention alphabet) Heidi Swapp; (butterfly, pink/copper border) SEI *Font:* (CK Holiday Spirit) Creating Keepsakes *Tool:* (corner rounder punch) Marvy Uchida **Finished size: 6" x 3½"**

5 STEPS Girlfriend Card   Designer: Teri Anderson

❶ Make card from cardstock. ❷ Cut patterned paper slightly smaller than card front. Affix border sticker. ❸ Print sentiment on cardstock. Trim and adhere to piece. ❹ Spell "Girlfriend" with stickers. Affix butterfly. ❺ Round one corner and adhere finished piece to card.

Sunday Pie Brenda Peterson

Sunday Pie has been a family tradition for as long as I can remember. It is easy to make and is also very versatile. I have made it for Sunday dinner dessert, as well as dressed it up with chocolate shavings and put fresh berries on top for a dinner party.

INGREDIENTS

1 c. flour
1 cube butter
1 tbsp. sugar
1 tbsp. vanilla flavoring
1 pkg. (8 oz.) cream cheese
1 c. Cool Whip topping
1 c. powdered sugar
1 small box chocolate instant pudding
1 small box vanilla instant pudding
2½ c. cold milk

DIRECTIONS Mix flour, butter, sugar, and vanilla flavoring together with pastry blender. Sprinkle into 9" x 13" baking pan and press. Bake at 350 degrees for 20 minutes. Cool.

In medium bowl, mix cream cheese, Cool Whip topping, and powdered sugar together. Spread over cooled crust.

In large bowl, mix chocolate pudding, vanilla pudding, and milk together until pudding is thick. Spread over cream cheese/Cool Whip topping layer. Refrigerate 1 to 2 hours before serving.

Serving suggestions: Top with Cool Whip topping, chocolate shavings, and/or fresh berries.

YIELDS APPROX. 16-24 SERVINGS.

Father's Day Card & Photo Cube

Designer: Jessica Witty

CARD 1 Make card from cardstock. 2 Adhere patterned paper. 3 Cut strips of patterned paper; staple together. Sand edges and adhere. 4 Stamp It's Good To Be King on cardstock. Trim, mat with patterned paper, sand edges, and adhere. 5 Tie ribbon on clip. Attach clip to card. 6 Write "Happy Father's Day" with marker.

PHOTO BLOCK 1 In software, crop and resize five photos to 3½" square. Print photos on specialty paper. Trim, sand edges, and adhere to block. 2 Cut square of patterned paper. Sand edges and adhere to block. 3 Embellish as desired with stickers, ribbon, and patterned paper strips. 4 Write sentiment and names using marker.

DESIGNER TIP

Since the Front Porch collection is no longer available from My Mind's Eye, try substituting this paper with a similar green plaid patterned paper.

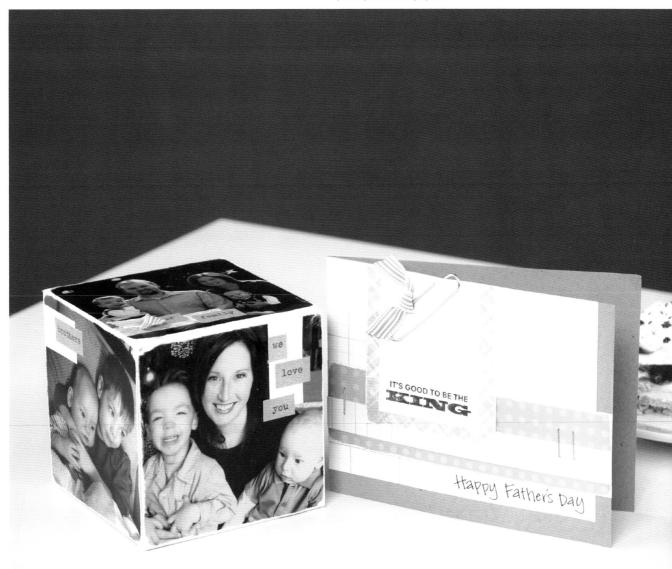

SUPPLIES: *Cardstock:* (Whisper White, kraft) Stampin' Up! *Patterned paper:* (Grey Grid on White, Worn Lined from Background collection) Scenic Route; (Organized One Word from Choices I collection) KI Memories; (Fresh Linens Green Plaid from Front Porch collection) My Mind's Eye *Specialty paper:* (photo) *Rubber stamps:* (It's Good to Be King) Inkadinkado *Dye ink:* (Bashful Blue, Chocolate Chip) Stampin' Up! *Color medium:* (brown marker) *Accents:* (paper clip, silver staples) *Stickers:* (kraft words) Making Memories *Fibers:* (green/white striped ribbon) May Arts *Software:* (photo editing) *Adhesive:* (decoupage) Plaid *Other:* (block) **Finished sizes: card 5½" x 4¾", photo block 3½" cube**

SUPPLIES: *Cardstock:* (Petunia, Truffle, white) Bazzill Basics Paper *Patterned paper:* (Thankful from Thankful collection) Melissa Frances *Pigment ink:* (Dusty Plum) Clearsnap *Chalk ink:* (Chestnut Roan) Clearsnap *Accents:* (sentiment) Melissa Frances; (brown buttons) BasicGrey *Adhesive:* (foam tape)
Finished size: 5½" x 4¾"

Over & Above Card Designer: Heather Thompson

① Make card from cardstock. Distress and ink edges. ② Cut square of patterned paper. Ink edges and adhere. ③ Adhere cardstock strip. ④ Cut flowers from patterned paper. Ink edges and adhere. *Note: Only adhere flower centers so the flower edges curl up.* ⑤ Ink edges of sentiment. Mat with cardstock and adhere with foam tape. ⑥ Adhere buttons.

DESIGNER TIPS

• Use cat-eye shaped ink pads to make inking curved edges easy.

• Extending your design above the top of your card not only adds dimension, but also allows the card to still stand up on its own.

Mint Chocolate Frozen Dessert Wendy Gallamore

This is a variation of a dessert recipe that I had at a book group meeting.

INGREDIENTS

½ gallon chocolate chip mint ice cream
1 pkg. Oreo cookies
⅓ c. sugar
½ c. melted butter or margarine
1 jar (16 oz.) hot fudge
1 tub (8 oz.) Cool Whip topping

DIRECTIONS Set ice cream out to soften. Crush cookies; mix with melted butter or margarine and sugar. Spread in 9" x 13" pan and freeze 20 minutes, reserving 1 c. of mixture. Spread hot fudge over crust (let stand in hot water 10 minutes to soften). Freeze 20 minutes. Spread ice cream over hot fudge; freeze 20 minutes. Spread Cool Whip on top. Drizzle hot fudge and sprinkle remaining crumb mixture over the top. Freeze until ready to serve.

SUPPLIES: *Cardstock:* (white) The Paper Company *Patterned paper:* (green polka dot) *Pigment ink:* (Green) Clearsnap *Paint:* (yellow) Delta *Accents:* (green felt shamrocks, shamrock brads) Queen & Co.; (yellow, green rhinestones) Darice; (chipboard oval, cloud, label) BasicGrey; (yellow glitter) Doodlebug Design *Stickers:* (Loopy Lou alphabet) Doodlebug Design *Fibers:* (green grosgrain ribbon) Michaels *Font:* (Typo Upright) www.myfonts.com *Adhesive:* (foam tape) *Die:* (tag) Provo Craft *Tools:* (die cut machine) Provo Craft; (½", 1½", 2" circle punch) *Other:* (gable box) Emma's Paperie
Finished sizes: pocket card 4¼" x 5", pocket card tag 3¾" x 5½", gift box 4" x 5½" x 2½"

:5: St. Patrick's Day Party   Designer: Anabelle O'Malley

POCKET CARD ❶ Cut two squares of cardstock. Punch half circle in one square. Ink edges. Adhere squares together on three sides to form pocket. ❷ Cut patterned paper slightly smaller than pocket card front; adhere. *Note: Punch half circle in patterned paper prior to adhering.* ❸ Paint chipboard label and apply glitter; let dry. Adhere. ❹ Adhere felt shamrocks, brads, and rhinestones. ❺ Spell "Join us" with stickers. ❻ Print party information on cardstock. Trim into tag and ink edges. ❼ Punch hole in tag. Tie with ribbon. ❽ Attach brad to felt shamrock. Adhere. ❾ Adhere rhinestone. Insert tag in pocket.

GIFT BOX ❶ Cover box sides with patterned paper. ❷ Paint chipboard cloud; apply glitter and let dry. Adhere. ❸ Tie ribbon around box. Attach brads to felt shamrocks; adhere. Adhere rhinestones. ❹ Print "Leprechaun kisses" on cardstock. Die-cut into tag. Ink edges. ❺ Attach brad to felt shamrock; adhere to tag. Adhere rhinestone. Adhere tag to box.

DESIGNER TIP

When adding glitter to painted chipboard, use the same color of glitter as the paint. This will ensure a more vibrant color on your finished project.

① Fold cardstock in half; cut circle card. ② Cut 6¼" and slightly smaller circles from patterned paper; layer and adhere. ③ Cut patterned paper strips; adhere. ④ Punch circles from cardstock to make bear. Assemble and adhere. Cut patterned paper pieces to make hat. Adhere. ⑤ Spell sentiment with rub-ons and stickers.

DESIGNER TIPS

• Transform the polar bear into a lion by changing the color and adding a paper strip mane.

• Change the word "cool" to "wild" and change the colors of the card to match your favorite wild dessert.

SUPPLIES: *Cardstock:* (Pear, Lily White, Ebony) Bazzill Basics Paper *Patterned paper:* (In Love from Crush collection, Claire from Sweet Pea collection) Fancy Pants Designs; (Corteza from Madera Island collection) SEI *Rub-on:* (Simply Sweet alphabet) Doodlebug Design *Stickers:* (Newsprint alphabet) Heidi Swapp *Tools:* (circle cutter; ⅛", 1 ½" circle punches) **Finished size: 6¼" diameter**

Peach Pie Stacy Croninger

This pie is a combination of two recipes—apple and peach pie. The great thing about this pie is it can be made year round with frozen peaches. Nothing is as comforting as warm pie with ice cream!

INGREDIENTS

5 c. sliced fresh or frozen peaches
1 c. sugar
Pie crust for single-crust pie
½ c. flour
½ tsp. cinnamon
¼ tsp. ginger
½ tsp. cardamom
¼ c. butter, softened

DIRECTIONS

Combine ½ c. sugar and peaches; mix until coated. Pour into 9" unbaked pie crust. Combine remaining sugar and spices. Cut in butter; mix until mixture is crumbly. Sprinkle over peaches. Cover edges of pie crust with foil. Bake pie at 375 degrees for 30 minutes. Remove foil. Bake for another 30 minutes or until topping is golden. Serve warm with vanilla ice cream.

U R a Peach Card
Designer: Kim Hughes

ACCENT PIECE ❶ Cut peach shape from adhesive sheet. ❷ Peel backing from one side and apply to cardstock. Cut around peach shape. ❸ Peel backing from remaining side; apply flock. *Note: Press the flock powder into the image and rub off excess.* ❹ Ink peach edges. ❺ Spell "Peach" on patterned paper with stickers. Trim and adhere.

CARD *Sand all paper and die cut edges.* ❶ Make card from patterned paper. ❷ Cut patterned paper smaller than card front. Stamp Spanish Script Backgrounder. Mat with patterned paper; adhere. ❸ Spell "U r a" with stickers. ❹ Attach brad to flower die cut; adhere. ❺ Adhere accent piece and peach stem/leaves.

DESIGNER TIP

Give your peach added dimension by lightly inking the edges with the Pumpkin Patch ink and then adding the Chestnut Roan ink.

SUPPLIES: *Cardstock:* (peach) *Patterned paper:* (Primrose, Vineyard from Fleuriste collection) Cosmo Cricket *Rubber stamp:* (Spanish Script Backgrounder) Cornish Heritage Farms *Chalk ink:* (Chestnut Roan, Pumpkin Patch) Clearsnap *Accents:* (white velvet flock) Doodlebug Design; (flower, stem, leaves die cuts) Cosmo Cricket; (red brad) *Stickers:* (Recess alphabet, Sweets alphabet) BasicGrey; (Fleuriste alphabet) Cosmo Cricket *Adhesive:* (double-sided sheet) Therm O Web **Finished size: 4½" x 5½"**

SUPPLIES: *Cardstock:* (Kiwi) Prism *Patterned paper:* (Building A Home, Look Around, She's Not Alone, Sing Just Enough from Birdie Bits collection) Dream Street Papers *Chalk ink:* (Charcoal, Chestnut Roan) Clearsnap *Color medium:* (black pen) *Accents:* (red buttons) Making Memories *Stickers:* (Shimmer alphabet) Making Memories *Fibers:* (green grosgrain ribbon) Offray; (red floss) DMC **Finished sizes: pie wrap 23½" x 4", tag 2¾" x 4¾"**

Peach Pie Wrap & Tag Designer: Melanie Douthit

PIE WRAP ❶ Cut two 12" x 1¾" strips of cardstock and two 12" x 1½" strips of patterned paper. Ink edges. Layer and adhere strips together to make 23½" long strip. ❷ Cut flowers and leaves from patterned paper. Ink edges. ❸ Adhere leaves. Layer and adhere flowers. ❹ Stitch buttons with floss; adhere.

TAG ❶ Make tag from cardstock. Cover tag front with patterned paper; ink edges. ❷ Trim bird from patterned paper.

Adhere. Draw legs with pen. ❸ Spell "For you" with stickers. ❹ Punch hole in tag. Tie tag to pie wrap with ribbon.

Old Fashioned Apple Dumplings Courtesy of AllRecipes.com

This old-fashioned dessert is the perfect ending to any meal!

INGREDIENTS

1 double pie crust
6 large Granny Smith apples, peeled and cored
½ c. butter
¾ c. brown sugar
1 tsp. ground cinnamon
½ tsp. ground nutmeg
3 c. water
2 c. white sugar
1 tsp. vanilla extract

DIRECTIONS Preheat oven to 400 degrees. Butter a 9" x 13" pan. On a lightly floured surface, roll pastry into a large rectangle, about 24" x 16". Cut into 6 square pieces. Place an apple on each pastry square with the cored opening facing upward. Cut butter into 8 pieces. Place 1 piece of butter in the opening of each apple; reserve remaining butter for sauce. Divide brown sugar between apples, poking some inside each cored opening and the rest around the base of each apple. Sprinkle cinnamon and nutmeg over apples.

With slightly wet fingertips, bring one corner of pastry square up to the top of the apple, then bring the opposite corner to the top and press together. Bring up the two remaining corners and seal. Slightly pinch the dough at the sides to completely seal in the apple. Repeat with remaining apples. Place completed apple dumplings in prepared baking dish.

In a saucepan, combine water, white sugar, vanilla extract, and reserved butter. Place over medium heat and bring to a boil in a large saucepan. Boil for 5 minutes, or until sugar is dissolved. Carefully pour over dumplings.

Bake 50 to 60 minutes. Place each dumpling in a dessert bowl and spoon sauce over the top.

Paper Crafts Gourmet **93**

SUPPLIES: *Cardstock:* (kraft) *Patterned paper:* (Home Room from Recess collection) BasicGrey; (Winter Birds from Winter Garden collection) Creative Imaginations *Dye ink:* (Black Soot) Ranger Industries *Paint:* (black) Delta *Accents:* (chipboard +) BasicGrey; (chipboard A) The Paper Studio; (black brads) Making Memories; (black eyelet) Pebbles Inc. *Rub-on:* (teacher) Heidi Swapp *Fibers:* (black criss-cross grosgrain ribbon) Offray; (orange yarn) SEI *Other:* (ramekin, cellophane wrap) **Finished size: 4¼" x 5"**

5 steps A+ Teacher Tag Designer: Summer Ford

❶ Cut apple, following pattern on p. 175. ❷ Trim patterned paper apples and adhere to cardstock apple. Ink and stitch edges. ❸ Paint chipboard A and +. Adhere. ❹ Apply rub-on. Attach brads and set eyelet. ❺ Wrap ramekin with cellophane. Attach tag to cellophane with fibers.

COVER ❶ Print sentiment on patterned paper. Trim and mat with cardstock. Adhere to album cover. ❷ Spell "Apple" with stickers. ❸ Adhere leaves. ❹ Attach brad to crochet flower. Adhere.

INSIDE ❶ Cut square of patterned paper slightly smaller than album page. Adhere. ❷ Adhere photos. *Note: Punch holes in pictures and insert in binder rings prior to adhering.* ❸ Print children's names on patterned paper, trim, and adhere. ❹ Tie ribbon.

Inside

SUPPLIES: *Cardstock:* (Ruby Red) Bazzill Basics Paper *Patterned paper:* (Starburst, Sunshine, Magpie, Sprout from Magpie collection) Scrapworks *Accents:* (yellow crochet flower) Fancy Pants Designs; (felt leaves) Creative Impressions; (red velvet brad) Making Memories *Stickers:* (Jewelry Box alphabet) American Crafts *Fibers:* (green gingham, red ribbon) May arts; (yellow striped/red stitched ribbon) BasicGrey *Font:* (Doodleonomy Fred) www.abstractfonts.com *Other:* (scalloped acrylic album) Scrapworks; (photos) **Finished size: 6" square**

Death by Chocolate Fondue Pattie Donham

Just the thought of liquid chocolate makes my mouth water. I like to use both milk chocolate and semi-sweet chocolate bits so that everyone's chocolate preference is satiated. And, when you add the whipping cream and liqueur, the texture is so silky it will make you swoon!

INGREDIENTS

1 pkg. (11 oz.) Ghirardelli semi-sweet chocolate bits
1 pkg. (11 oz.) Ghirardelli milk chocolate bits
½ pint whipping cream
½ c. Kahlua liqueur

DIRECTIONS Place chocolate bits in a large bowl, and pour cream and liqueur over chocolate, stirring it in. Melt slowly in a microwave, stirring frequently with a wood spoon until melted. Pour into a fondue pot, and light the flame underneath the pot to keep it warm.

Serve with marshmallows, crushed graham crackers, strawberries, crushed nuts, pineapple and apple chunks, and/or shredded coconut.

INVITATION ❶ Make card from cardstock. ❷ Cut patterned paper slightly smaller than card front. Adhere paper trim; adhere piece. ❸ Print sentiment on cardstock. Trim and adhere. ❹ Attach brad to paper flower; adhere.

PARTY MEMORIES BOOKLET

Prepare Cut rectangle of cardstock. Tri-fold to create booklet.

Cover ❶ Cut patterned paper slightly smaller than booklet front; adhere. ❷ Print title on cardstock. Trim and adhere. ❸ Attach brad to paper flower. Adhere.

Inside ❶ Print questions on cardstock. Trim and adhere. ❷ Cut cardstock slightly smaller than booklet section. Adhere. ❸ Adhere paper trim to backside of two patterned paper strips. Adhere. ❹ Print booklet section titles on cardstock. Trim and adhere.

PLACE HOLDER ❶ Cut cardstock to finished size. ❷ Cut patterned paper slightly smaller; adhere. ❸ Print guest name on cardstock. Trim and mat with paper trim. Adhere. ❹ Adhere smiley face patch with foam tape.

SUPPLIES: *Cardstock:* (Lily White, Lilac, Lemon Drop) Bazzill Basics Paper *Patterned paper:* (Summer Scallop from Summer Crush collection) Glitz Design *Accents:* (pink corduroy brads) Imaginisce; (pink paper flowers) Prima; (purple paper trim) Doodlebug Design *Fonts:* (Bell Bottom Laser) www.dafont.com; (your choice) *Adhesive:* (foam tape) *Other:* (smiley face patch) **Finished sizes: invitation 4½" x 5½", party memories booklet 11" x 6", place holder 4¾" x 4¾"**

SUPPLIES: *Cardstock:* (white) Bazzill Basics Paper; (brown) Prism *Patterned paper:* (Front Porch, Courtyard, Window Box from Summer Cottage collection; Surfboard from Under the Boardwalk collection) Daisy Bucket Designs *Rubber stamps:* (lips, strawberry, scalloped heart, swirl heart, ladybug from Hugs and Kisses set) Cornish Heritage Farms *Watermark ink:* Tsukineko *Chalk ink:* (Dark Brown) Clearsnap *Embossing powder:* (Chocoholic Brownie) Cornish Heritage Farms *Color medium:* (light green pen) Sakura *Font:* (Mademoiselle) www.twopeasinabucket.com *Tools:* (½", ¾" circle punches) EK Success **Finished sizes: card 4¼" x 5½", place mat 12" x 12", napkin wrap 5¾" x 1"**

:5: Sweet Treat Ensemble Designer: Kim Hughes

ACCENT PIECES ❶ Trim two flowers and punch ten multi-sized circles from patterned papers. ❷ Stamp hearts, lips, and three strawberries on patterned paper; trim. ❸ Emboss strawberries and hearts. Color strawberry leaves with pen.

CARD ❶ Make card from cardstock. ❷ Cut patterned paper slightly smaller than card front; adhere. ❸ Print sentiment on cardstock. Trim and adhere. ❹ Adhere patterned paper. *Note: Trim one edge in wave.* Stitch edges. ❺ Adhere wavy strip of patterned paper over paper seams. ❻ Adhere accent pieces.

PLACE MAT ❶ Cut patterned paper slightly smaller than cardstock. Adhere. Stitch edges. ❷ Cut wavy strip of patterned paper. Adhere. ❸ Adhere accent pieces.

NAPKIN WRAP ❶ Cut strip of patterned paper. Stitch edges. Adhere ends together. ❷ Adhere accent pieces.

From parties and place settings to a thoughtful card and meal for someone who could use a helping hand, you'll find great paper-crafting projects to go with this selection of main dish recipes.

MAIN DISHES

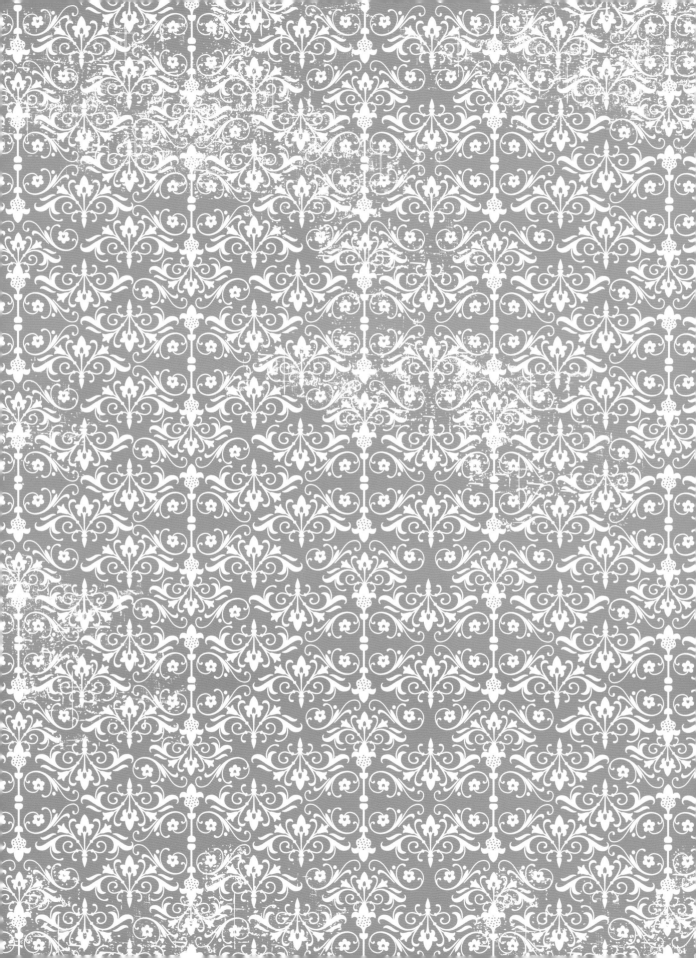

Louisiana Gumbo Melanie Douthit

I was led to believe gumbo was something complicated to make, and as I learned to make it, I realized that wasn't true. I usually make this at least twice a month and my family loves it. It's inexpensive to make and, according to my husband, better than what you can get in a restaurant.

INGREDIENTS

1 lb. deboned chicken breasts
1 lb. smoked sausage
¼ - ⅓ c. vegetable oil
1 medium onion, chopped
½ bell pepper, chopped
3 stalks celery, chopped
1 can (6 oz.) okra and tomatoes mix
½ c. chopped green onions
Tony Chachere's Creole Seasonings to taste
Salt and pepper to taste
½ tsp. crushed red pepper
¼ c. all purpose flour
Stock from chicken
Gumbo file (optional)

DIRECTIONS Boil chicken breasts on low heat until cooked through. Reserve stock. When cooled, chop chicken into bite size pieces; set aside. Slice smoked sausage and place in cooking pan with 1 tsp. vegetable oil. Cook until browned, stirring frequently. Drain on paper towels. Place chicken in same pan used for sausage. Cook chicken for 1 to 2 minutes, stirring frequently. Remove. In large dutch oven, add onion, green pepper, and celery along with approx. 1 tbsp. oil; sauté until tender. Remove from pan. To make roux, add remaining oil to pan. Add flour. Cook over medium heat stirring constantly until mixture is caramel colored, but do not burn.

Add onion, green pepper, and celery to roux. Add chicken broth (approx. 4 c.); stir frequently. Add sausage, chicken, and seasonings. Bring to boil. Reduce heat and simmer. In small blender, blend ½ of the canned okra tomatoes mix. Add to gumbo. Continue to cook for 1½ to 2 hours on low heat. Do not use a lid. Add more water to pot if gumbo seems too thick. Add chopped green onions the last 10 to 15 minutes of cooking. Add file right before serving. Serve over hot cooked rice.

SUPPLIES: Cardstock: (black) Patterned paper: (Lovely Lace from First Blush collection) Paper Salon Rubber stamps: (frame from Monogram Builder II set, for you from Wedding Essentials set) Paper Salon Watermark ink: Ranger Industries Embossing powder: (gold) Ranger Industries Accents: (black safety pin) Making Memories; (black feathers) Fibers: (black organza ribbon) Offray; (black sequin trim) Font: (Freehand 521) www.myfonts.com Adhesive: (foam tape) Template: (pillow box) C&T Publishing Die: (photo corner) Provo Craft Tool: (die cut machine) Provo Craft Other: (black decorative netting, gold, green, purple bead necklaces, gold coins) Finished sizes: card 4½" x 5¾", gift box 5¾" x 3¼" x 1", mask 8¾" x 3"

Mardi Gras Party Designer: Melanie Douthit

CARD ❶ Make card from cardstock. ❷ Adhere decorative netting to patterned paper piece. Adhere trim; tie with ribbon. Adhere to card. ❸ Print invitation on patterned paper; trim and mat with cardstock. ❹ Die-cut photo corners from cardstock; emboss and adhere. ❺ Adhere with foam tape.

GIFT BOX ❶ Trace pillow box template onto patterned paper; cut out and assemble. ❷ Adhere decorative netting. Adhere trim; tie with ribbon. ❸ Stamp frame and for you on

cardstock; emboss and trim. ❹ Attach to ribbon with safety pin. ❺ Fill with necklaces and coins.

MASK ❶ Cut mask, following pattern on p. 176. ❷ Adhere trim and feathers to patterned paper mask. ❸ Mount on cardstock mask.

SUPPLIES: *Cardstock:* (Chantilly, blue) Bazzill Basics Paper *Patterned paper:* (Snowflake Garden from Frost Blvd. collection) Heidi Grace Designs *Dye ink:* (Taken with Teal) Stampin' Up! *Accents:* (boy, dog die cuts; boy, dog chipboard) BasicGrey; (brown buttons) Magic Scraps *Rub-on:* (flourish) Tinkering Ink *Fibers:* (light blue rickrack) Wrights *Font:* (Bernhard Fashion HMK) Hallmark Connections *Tool:* (water brush) *Other:* (dimensional glaze) Stampin' Up! **Finished size: 9" x 4"**

Ice Skating Party Designer: Wendy Johnson

ACCENT PIECES ❶ Adhere boy and dog die cut pieces to coordinating chipboard pieces. ❷ Adhere rickrack and buttons.

CARD ❶ Make card from cardstock. Set aside. ❷ Cut rectangle of patterned paper size of card front. Ink edges. Cut slit for interactive element. Apply rub-on. ❸ Adhere cardstock strip to patterned paper piece. Apply dimensional glaze. Let dry. ❹ Tear cardstock strips for snowbanks. Adhere. ❺ Print party information on cardstock. Trim and adhere to back of boy accent piece. Insert interactive strip in slit. ❻ Adhere dog accent piece. ❼ Adhere patterned paper piece to card. *Note: Do not adhere space around interactive element.*

Apricot-Curry Chicken
Wendy Gallamore

This recipe is a rendition of a dish a friend brought over when our son, Davis, was born.

INGREDIENTS

4 - 6 boneless, skinless chicken breasts
3 tbsp. flour
1 tbsp. curry powder
1½ tsp. salt
4 tbsp. vegetable oil
2 tbsp. brown sugar
1 small onion, sliced
2 chicken bouillon cubes
1 c. water
1 jar (7¾ oz.) apricot baby food
½ tbsp. lemon juice
1 tsp. soy sauce
1 can (8¾ oz.) apricot halves

DIRECTIONS

Combine flour, curry powder, and salt in large resealable bag. Add chicken and shake to coat. Brown chicken lightly in vegetable oil over medium heat. Place chicken in large baking dish coated with non-stick spray. Stir into drippings sugar, bouillon, water, apricot baby food, lemon juice, soy sauce, and onion. Heat to boiling; pour over chicken. Bake at 350 degrees for 35 minutes or until chicken is tender. Place chicken in serving dish. Add cornstarch to sauce to thicken; pour over chicken. Add apricot halves to garnish.

INVITATION ❶ Cut patterned paper to finished size; punch sides. ❷ Adhere patterned paper. ❸ Spell "Admit one" with stickers. ❹ Write party details on back.

BALLOT ❶ Make card from patterned paper. ❷ Adhere slightly smaller patterned paper piece. ❸ Punch circles from patterned paper; adhere. ❹ Spell "Ballot" with stickers.

TREAT BOXES ❶ Die-cut 4½" boxes from cardstock; assemble. ❷ Punch circles from patterned paper; adhere.

DESIGNER TIP

Print award categories on cardstock and adhere inside the ballots. Leave enough space for party guests to write in their choices before the show begins.

SUPPLIES: *Cardstock:* (white) *Patterned paper:* (Peace, Vivid, Rockin' from About a Boy collection) Fancy Pants Designs *Stickers:* (Hopscotch alphabet) Doodlebug Design *Die:* (popcorn box) Provo Craft *Tools:* (die cut machine) Provo Craft; (assorted circle punches) EK Success **Finished sizes: invitation 4½" x 3½", ballot 4¼" x 5¼", treat boxes 3" x 4½" x 3"**

SUPPLIES: *Cardstock:* (Very Vanilla, Chocolate Chip) Stampin' Up! *Patterned paper:* (Madison, Hazel, Taylor) Melissa Frances *Clear stamps:* (daisy from Floral Frenzy set) Lizzie Anne Designs *Dye ink:* (Chocolate Chip) Stampin' Up! *Solvent ink:* (Jet Black) Tsukineko *Color medium:* (brown marker) Stampin' Up! *Accents:* (white buttons) Melissa Frances *Fibers:* (linen thread) Stampin' Up!; (brown ruffled ribbon) May Arts *Adhesive:* (foam tape) *Tools:* (blender pen; 1⅜", 1", ⅝" circle punches) Stampin' Up! *Other:* (copper wire) **Finished sizes: place mat 17" x 12", napkin ring 2" width, wine charms 1" diameter**

Woven Place Setting
5 STEPS

Designer: Lindsey Botkin

PLACE MAT ❶ Adhere cardstock together to make mat. ❷ Cut 12" x 1½" strips of patterned paper. Cut 12" x ½" strips of cardstock. ❸ Weave strips together; adhere to mat. Adhere cardstock strip. ❹ Stamp daisies; watercolor. Cut out and adhere. ❺ Adhere ribbon. Tie buttons with thread; adhere.

NAPKIN RING ❶ Cut cardstock strip. Pierce edges; draw stitches. ❷ Adhere patterned paper strip. Adhere strip ends to form ring. ❸ Cut cardstock strip; trim ends and adhere.

Punch circle from cardstock; adhere. ❹ Stamp daisy; watercolor. Cut out and adhere with foam tape.

WINE CHARMS ❶ Punch circles from cardstock. Punch circles from patterned paper; adhere. ❷ Pierce top of charms; thread with wire. Curl wire ends. ❸ Stamp daisies; watercolor. Cut out and adhere.

DESIGNER TIP

Adhere an extra cardstock circle to the back of the wine charms for added sturdiness.

Sticky Chicken Cindy Schow

A friend shared this recipe with me a few months back and it has quickly become one of our family favorites. It's quick and easy to put together with very few ingredients and the best part is that it tastes really good! We like to serve it over rice and have a green salad on the side.

INGREDIENTS

½ c. Kraft Russian salad dressing
½ c. apricot jam
½ envelope Lipton onion soup mix
1 tsp. curry powder
10 - 12 boneless skinless chicken thighs

DIRECTIONS

Arrange chicken pieces in a roaster pan. Mix first four ingredients well and pour over chicken pieces. Cover and bake at 350 degrees for approx. 1½ hours, until tender. Pull chicken apart into small bite-size pieces and mix into sauce. Serve over rice.

SUPPLIES: *Patterned paper:* (Bright Floral, Bright Polka Dot from C'est la Vie collection) My Mind's Eye; (Non-fat Yogurt from Two Scoops collection) BasicGrey *Dye ink:* (Old Paper) Ranger Industries *Accents:* (white, clear buttons) Melissa Frances; (blue felt, cream paper flowers) Making Memories; (red plaid fabric) *Rub-ons:* (Ginger alphabet) American Crafts *Fibers:* (tan twill ribbon) Wrights; (red floss) Martha Stewart Crafts; (aqua grosgrain ribbon) *Font:* (Times New Roman) Microsoft *Die:* (heart bookplate) Provo Craft *Tools:* (decorative-edge scissors, die cut machine) Provo Craft *Other:* (album) Junkitz **Finished size: 9" x 6"**

Family Reunion Recipes Book Designer: Melissa Phillips

BOOKPLATE ❶ Die-cut 4" bookplate from patterned paper; sand edges. ❷ Adhere fabric behind bookplate; stitch opening edge with floss. ❸ Spell "Family recipes" with rub-ons. ❹ Stitch buttons to bookplate with floss.

COVER ❶ Cut patterned paper to fit cover. Adhere patterned paper strip; ink edges. ❷ Trim patterned paper strip with decorative-edge scissors; punch edge. Ink edges and adhere. ❸ Stitch edges, tie with ribbon, and adhere. ❹ Adhere bookplate. Stitch flowers and button with floss; adhere.

INSIDE ❶ Trim patterned paper strips with decorative-edge scissors; punch edges and adhere to patterned paper pieces. ❷ Ink edges of patterned paper pieces; adhere. *Note: Tie ribbon around one piece before adhering.* ❸ Print recipe on patterned paper; trim. Ink edges and adhere. ❹ Stitch flowers and buttons with floss; adhere.

DESIGNER TIP

Collect family favorite recipes from attendees in advance and include them in each family's copy of this recipe book.

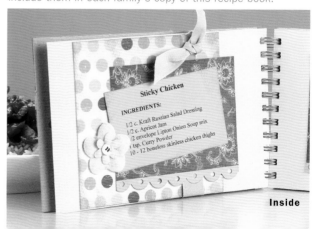

Sticky Chicken

INGREDIENTS:

1/2 c. Kraft Russian Salad Dressing
1/2 c. Apricot Jam
1/2 envelope Lipton Onion Soup mix
1 tsp. Curry Powder
10 - 12 boneless skinless chicken thighs

Inside

Homespun Get Well Card
Designer: Nichol Magouirk

1 Cut patterned paper slightly smaller than card front.
2 Adhere patterned paper strips; round corners. 3 Adhere patterned paper strip; attach brads. 4 Punch circles from patterned paper; ink edges and adhere. 5 Stamp dotted circle. Spell sentiment with rub-ons. 6 Attach flowers with brads. Adhere piece to card.

DESIGNER TIP

This lovely card—accompanied by a meal she didn't have to cook—would make a thoughtful gift for a mom who's been under the weather.

SUPPLIES: *Patterned paper:* (Devoted, Pure, Sincere, Natural from True collection) Fancy Pants Designs *Rubber stamp:* (dotted circle from Round Grunge self-inking set) 7gypsies *Dye ink:* (brown) Ranger Industries *Accents:* (black, blue, cream brads; green, orange flowers) *Rub-ons:* (alphabet) Making Memories *Tools:* (1¾", 1" circle; corner rounder punches) EK Success *Other:* (brown card) Creative Café **Finished size: 4¼" x 5½"**

Chicken-Bean Burritos Alisa Bangerter

I really like Mexican food and I was trying to find a recipe that had something unique. When I first tried this recipe I was excited and my family loved it. I love food to be colorful and to look good on the plate when I serve it. This dish has really nice colors with the mix of ingredients and is part of the reason I like to make it for my family.

INGREDIENTS

2 - 3 boneless, skinless chicken breasts
1 can (15 oz.) black beans, drained and rinsed
1 c. cooked rice
½ c. frozen kernel corn
2 c. shredded cheddar or Monterey Jack cheese
2 c. mild or medium salsa
1 tsp. chili powder
½ tsp. salt
Pinch black pepper
12 (8") flour tortillas
½ c. chopped green onions

DIRECTIONS Boil chicken breasts until chicken is tender. Let cool and cut into small pieces. Combine chicken, beans, rice, and corn. Stir in 1 c. of cheese and 1 c. of salsa. Add chili powder, salt, and pepper, and mix well. Place approximately ⅓ c. of filling down the center of each tortilla and roll up. Place tortillas in a greased 9" x 13" baking dish. Spread remaining salsa down the center of the tortillas. Cover with foil and bake for 20 minutes at 375 degrees. Remove from oven and sprinkle with remaining cheese. Bake, uncovered, at 425 degrees for 10 to 15 minutes longer, or until heated through and cheese is melted. Sprinkle with chopped green onions. Gently pull apart each burrito to serve.

YIELDS 6-8 SERVINGS.

INVITATION ❶ Cover small clipboard with patterned paper. ❷ Print invitation on cardstock; trim. Mat with cardstock; secure under clip. ❸ Affix basketball stickers to invitation and tag. ❹ Punch tag; attach to clip with chain. Tie ribbon to clip.

CLIPBOARD ❶ Cover large clipboard with patterned paper. ❷ Adhere patterned paper strip. Adhere ribbon over seam. ❸ Adhere license plate with foam tape. ❹ Affix basketball stickers to tag; punch and attach to clip with chain.

DESIGNER TIPS

Use the clipboard to display the March Madness statistics chart or to keep track of the teams. Or, if you're having a buffet or snacks, attach a menu to the clipboard.

SUPPLIES: *Cardstock:* (rust, cream) Bazzill Basics Paper *Patterned paper:* (On The Line, Basketball Key from Basketball collection) Karen Foster Design *Accents:* (metal-rimmed tags) Avery; (silver bead chains) Making Memories *Stickers:* (basketballs, license plate) Karen Foster Design *Fibers:* (black gingham ribbon) Offray *Font:* (CK Letterman) Creating Keepsakes *Adhesive:* (foam tape) *Tool:* (⅛" circle punch) *Other:* (small clipboard) Nicole Crafts; (large clipboard) **Finished sizes:** invitation 4" x 6¾", clipboard 9" x 12½"

SUPPLIES: *Cardstock:* (brown, white) *Patterned paper:* (Guitar Strips, Star Strips, Guitars, plaid from Rock Star collection) Die Cuts With a View *Accent:* (silver tag clip) *Stickers:* (Kennedy Jr. alphabet; Shoebox alphabet) American Crafts *Fibers:* (black grosgrain ribbon) May Arts *Font:* (CK Evolution) Creating Keepsakes *Tool:* (corner rounder punch) Marvy Uchida **Finished sizes: invitation 5" x 5½", backstage pass 4¾" x 3¼"**

⁙5⁙ American Idol Finale Party Designer: Teri Anderson

INVITATION ❶ Make card from cardstock. ❷ Cut patterned paper piece. Adhere patterned paper strips; round corners and adhere. ❸ Cut out guitars from patterned paper; adhere. ❹ Affix stickers. ❺ Print invitation on cardstock; trim. ❻ Adhere patterned paper strips; round corners and adhere inside card.

BACKSTAGE PASS ❶ Make pass from cardstock. ❷ Cut patterned paper strips; round corners and adhere. ❸ Print text on cardstock; trim and adhere. ❹ Affix stickers. ❺ Attach clip to pass. Tie with ribbon.

BONUS IDEA

Use a digital camera to take photos during the party. Print the photos and give them to guests at the end of the night.

It's time to hear Simon scowl,
Paula cheer and
Randy say, "Dog."

It's time to cheer for Carries, Clays and Rubens.
It's time to see who the next Sanjaya is.
It is that time of year.

It is "American Idol" time.

The Anderson's are hosting an Idol party.
7 p.m. Tuesday

We'll be eating, singing along and voting.
Bring your cell phone.

Inside

Three Cheese Chicken Casserole Alisa Bangerter

My son loves pasta so I was trying to find something that would be a quick one-dish meal that would also feed a growing teenage boy! I also needed a good recipe to take to neighbors or pot-luck dinners and this one worked perfectly.

INGREDIENTS

2 tbsp. butter or margarine
1 small onion, chopped
½ c. green pepper, chopped
2 cans (10¾ oz. each) cream of chicken soup
1 can (8 oz.) sliced mushrooms
1 jar (2 oz.) pimentos, chopped
½ tsp. dried basil
1 package (8 oz.) egg noodles, cooked and drained
3 - 4 c. cooked diced chicken
2 c. grated cheddar cheese
2 c. cottage cheese
½ c. grated Parmesan cheese
Dried bread crumbs (optional)

DIRECTIONS Sauté onion and pepper in butter or margarine until tender. Remove from the heat and add soup, mushrooms, pimentos, and basil. Set aside. Mix together noodles, chicken, cheddar cheese, cottage cheese, and Parmesan cheese. Pour soup mixture over noodle mixture and combine well. *Note: Amount of soup can be adjusted if you want the casserole more or less saucy.* Pour into a greased 9" x 13" baking dish. Bake, uncovered, at 350 degrees for 45 minutes or until bubbly. Sprinkle with bread crumbs, if desired, and bake 10 minutes longer.

YIELDS APPROX. 10 SERVINGS

SUPPLIES: *Cardstock:* (Natural Smooth) Prism *Patterned paper:* (Sheriff, Bull Rider, Chaps from Cowboy collection) Crate Paper *Rubber stamps:* (welcome baby, giraffe from Baby Love set) Cornish Heritage Farms *Dye ink:* (Linen, Mushroom, Pitch Black) Ranger Industries *Color media:* (tan, blue markers) Copic Marker; (tan chalk) Pebbles Inc. *Paint:* (white) Making Memories *Accents:* (silver round, star brads) Making Memories; (acrylic star) *Fibers:* (blue gingham ribbon) Stampin' Up!; (brown floss) DMC *Tool:* (circle cutter) **Finished size: 9¾" x 4"**

Bringing Home Baby Card Designer: Julia Stainton

❶ Make card from cardstock. ❷ Ink edges of patterned paper strips; adhere. Stitch along seam with floss. ❸ Paint acrylic star; let dry. Adhere. ❹ Stamp welcome, baby, and giraffe on cardstock. Color with markers and chalk. Cut out with circle cutter; chalk edges. ❺ Mat with patterned paper. Adhere ribbon, attach brads, and adhere.

DESIGNER TIP

Acrylic shapes stand out better when brushed with a bit of paint, sponged with ink, or stamped.

BONUS IDEA

Make a train of animals by attaching a series of animals on brad "wheels," linked together with ribbon.

Love is Eternal Sympathy Card Designer: Danielle Flanders

1 Make card from cardstock. **2** Cover card with patterned paper; ink edges. **3** Adhere border die cut behind front flap. **4** Attach brad to felt; adhere. Apply rub-ons.

DESIGNER TIP

Extend your sympathy and a helping hand to someone grieving the loss of a family member with this card and casserole.

SUPPLIES: *Cardstock:* (cream) *Patterned paper:* (Devoted from Crush collection) Fancy Pants Designs *Dye ink:* (brown) Ranger Industries *Accents:* (scalloped border die cut, felt love) Fancy Pants Designs; (pink heart brad) Making Memories *Rub-ons:* (is, eternal) Making Memories **Finished size: 4½" x 7¾"**

Swiss Steak
Peggy Hoeppner

I came up with this simple way of cooking Swiss steak because my family enjoyed the dish, but I found cutting up tomatoes, green peppers, and onions too time consuming. It dawned on me that canned stewed tomatoes contained the same ingredients, so I decided to try making the dish using this ingredient instead. The results were tasty, and I felt rewarded for my laziness—a win, win!

INGREDIENTS

One round steak (medium thickness)
2 cans (14.5 oz. each) stewed tomatoes
¾ lb. small red potatoes
¼ c. flour
Salt and pepper to taste
1 - 2 tbsp. cooking oil

DIRECTIONS Cut round steak into serving size pieces. Flour and pound each piece. Salt and pepper to taste.

Add cooking oil to skillet and brown steak.* When all pieces are browned, place them in a baking dish and pour stewed tomatoes over meat; cover baking dish. Place in a 375 degree oven, and cook for 1 to 1½ hours, until tender.

Cut potatoes into pieces. Add them to meat ½ hour before time to take the dish from the oven.

*Cooking suggestion:
Four cloves of garlic and one medium onion can be added to the skillet when browning the meat for added flavor.

INVITATION *Adhere all accents with foam tape.* ❶ Cut patterned paper slightly smaller than card front; round corners, distress edges, and adhere. ❷ Thread tag on ribbon and tie around card. Adhere tag. ❸ Cut panel from patterned paper. Distress edges, roll corners, and adhere. ❹ Print sentiment on cardstock; trim, bend, and roll corners. Adhere. ❺ Punch heart from chipboard. Cover with patterned paper, sand edges, and apply glitter. Adhere.

PLACE CARDS *Adhere all accents with foam tape.* ❶ Cut card to finished size. ❷ Cut patterned paper slightly smaller than card front; round corners, distress edges, and adhere. ❸ Print guest name on cardstock; trim, bend, and roll corners. Adhere. ❹ Punch heart from chipboard. Cover with patterned paper, sand edges, and apply glitter. Adhere.

VASE WRAP *Adhere all accents with foam tape.* ❶ Cut patterned paper to fit around vase; distress edges and adhere. ❷ Adhere bird scalloped circle. ❸ Print sentiment on cardstock; trim, bend, and roll corners. Adhere. ❹ Punch heart from chipboard. Cover with patterned paper, sand edges, and apply glitter. Adhere. ❺ Tie ribbon.

SUPPLIES: *Cardstock:* (white) *Patterned paper:* (Wallpaper, Valentines, Heart Filigree from First Blush collection) Paper Salon *Accent:* (clear glitter) Stampin' Up! *Stickers:* (bird scalloped circle, tag) Paper Salon *Fibers:* (silver organza ribbon) Michaels *Font:* (Stanzie JF) www.myfonts.com *Adhesive:* (decoupage) Plaid; (foam tape) *Tools:* (corner rounder, heart punches) EK Success *Other:* (pink shimmer scalloped cards) Paper Salon; (glass vase) Michaels; (chipboard) **Finished sizes: invitation 5½" x 4¾", place cards 2¾" x 2", vase wrap 15" x 4½"**

SUPPLIES: *Cardstock:* (white) *Patterned paper:* (Village Drive from Sumner collection) Scenic Route *Chalk ink:* (Chestnut Roan) Clearsnap *Paint:* (white) Plaid *Accents:* (large, small chipboard plaques) Li'l Davis Designs; (keyhole) Melissa Frances *Fibers:* (white grosgrain ribbon) Offray *Fonts:* (Adorable, Mom's Typewriter) www.dafont.com **Finished size: 4" x 6"**

5 STEPS Happy Remodeling Card Designer: Sherry Wright

❶ Make card from cardstock. Cover with patterned paper; curve top edge. Ink edges. ❷ Adhere ribbon. Paint large chipboard plaque; ink edges and adhere. ❸ Print "Happy remodeling" on cardstock; trim and adhere to small plaque. Ink edges and adhere. ❹ Adhere keyhole.

DESIGNER TIP

Remodeling projects can eliminate the time—or the ability, when re-doing the kitchen—for homeowners to cook for themselves. Help out with this card and the Swiss Steak.

Honey-Butter Mexican Shrimp Tacos Susan Neal

This recipe is such a winner for me. It combines two of my favorite foods: seafood and Mexican food. It's also a great party dinner; tasty, colorful, and fun! Melt in your mouth, sweet, and spicy.

SHRIMP INGREDIENTS

1 lb. large shrimp in shell
⅓ c. butter
⅓ c. honey
1 tbsp. cumin
1 tsp. chipotle (to taste)
1 tsp. salt
Fresh ground pepper

DIRECTIONS Clean and de-vein shrimp and cut into 3 pieces each (depending on how large they are). Sauté in hot butter until cooked through. Add rest of ingredients. Cook just before serving.

MANGO SALSA INGREDIENTS

3 medium tomatoes, diced
1 large mango, diced
½ bunch cilantro, chopped
1 white onion, chopped
2 tbsp. fresh lime juice
¼ c. sliced green onions
Salt and pepper to taste

DIRECTIONS Combine all ingredients and allow to marinate in juices for a couple of hours in fridge.

TOMATILLO DRESSING INGREDIENTS

1 c. buttermilk
1 c. mayonnaise
1 pkg. dry ranch buttermilk dressing
2 jalapenos (to taste)
2 tomatillos
½ bunch cilantro
2 cloves garlic
½ fresh lime juice

DIRECTIONS Add all ingredients to the blender and blend until smooth.

SUPPLIES: *Cardstock:* (orange, white) *Patterned paper:* (orange floral from Family Tree collection) My Mind's Eye *Accents:* (chipboard letter) BasicGrey; (orange eyelet) *Fibers:* (blue rickrack, brown floss) *Font:* (Filosofia Unicase) www.myfonts.com *Software:* (photo editing) *Tool:* (1" circle punch) *Other:* (kraft gift box, wire, orange tissue) **Finished sizes: invitation 4" x 5½", place card 3½" square, gift box 3½" x 6" x 3½"**

⁙5⁙ Mother's Day Luncheon Designer: Celeste Rockwood-Jones

INVITATION ❶ Make pocket from patterned paper. Punch notch in top. ❷ Print party information on cardstock; trim to fit in pocket. ❸ Create 2" circle in software. Create border, type "You are invited", and print on cardstock. Trim. ❹ Cut slit in top of insert, tie rickrack, and attach to circle with eyelet.

PLACE CARD ❶ Print guest name on cardstock; trim. ❷ Mat with rickrack. ❸ Make card from cardstock; adhere piece.

GIFT BOX ❶ Make tissue flower (see "How to Make Tissue Flower" on p. 175). ❷ Cover chipboard letter with patterned paper. ❸ Tie rickrack around box. Attach letter with floss. ❹ Adhere tissue flower.

To Heck with Winter Party Designer: Becky Olsen

INVITATION ❶ Cut patterned paper to finished size. ❷ Print invitation on cardstock; trim and adhere. ❸ Cut 12" x 1" cardstock strip. Cut surfboards from patterned paper; adhere to strip. ❹ Fold ends of strip and adhere to form band. ❺ Slide band over invitation.

NOTEBOOK ❶ Cover notebook with patterned paper. ❷ Write "Warm thoughts" on cardstock; trim and mat with patterned paper. Adhere. ❸ Cut palm tree from patterned paper; adhere.

CENTERPIECE ❶ Cover can with patterned paper. ❷ Trim waves strip from patterned paper; adhere. *Note: Do not adhere wave tops.* ❸ Cut surfboards from patterned paper; adhere with foam tape. ❹ Trim waves strip from patterned paper; adhere with foam tape. ❺ Cut flowers from patterned paper; punch holes and slide on straws. Insert straws in can.

FOOD PICKS ❶ Write names of dishes on cardstock; trim and mat with patterned paper. ❷ Adhere pieces to picks. ❸ Cut palm trees from patterned paper; adhere.

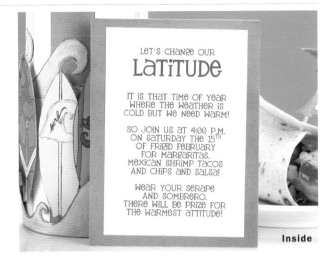

Inside

SUPPLIES: *Cardstock:* (orange, white) *Patterned paper:* (Surf's Up, Hibiscus, Beach Towel, Palm Trees from Boardwalk collection) Teresa Collins *Color medium:* (black pen) American Crafts *Font:* (Tangerine) www.scrapvillage.com *Adhesive:* (foam tape) Therm O Web *Other:* (notebook, can, plastic straws, wood picks) **Finished sizes: invitation 4¼" x 5½", notebook 3" x 5", centerpiece 3¾" diameter x 10" height, food picks 2½" x 3"**

Machaca Beef Kim Kesti

This is a yummy Mexican-style dish that cooks up in the crockpot with very little supervision. That leaves me with more time for paper crafting!

INGREDIENTS

1½ lbs. boneless beef roast
1 large onion, sliced
1 can (4 oz.) chopped green chiles
1 tbsp. minced garlic
1 can (28 oz.) chopped tomatoes
1 tsp. salt
½ tsp. cumin
1 tsp. fresh ground pepper

DIRECTIONS Place all ingredients in crockpot, cook on low for 8 to 10 hours. Remove beef from crockpot, set cooking liquid aside. Shred beef, using two forks. Chop remaining ingredients, if necessary, and mix back in with shredded beef.

Use beef for a variety of main dishes: burritos, tacos, enchiladas, chimichangas. Mostly, we like to roll the meat in a warmed tortilla with a dollop of sour cream and enjoy!

INVITATION ❶ Cut patterned paper to finished size. ❷ Print invitation on patterned paper; trim and adhere. ❸ Adhere snowflake tile.

UTENSIL CUP ❶ Adhere strip of patterned paper to cup. ❷ Adhere snowflake tile. ❸ Wrap utensils in napkin, tie with raffia, and place in cup.

FAVOR ❶ Print "Keep warm!" on patterned paper; trim. ❷ Apply rub-on. Adhere snowflake tile. ❸ Insert foot warmer in bag; staple topper.

SUPPLIES: *Patterned paper:* (Chatsworth, Bentley, Sudbury from Haberdasher collection) Tinkering Ink *Dye ink:* (Van Dyke Brown) Ranger Industries *Accents:* (felt/rubber snowflake tiles) Tinkering Ink; (staples) *Rub-on:* (hexagon border) Tinkering Ink *Font:* (Bernard MT Condensed) www.myfonts.com *Other:* (cellophane bag, paper cup, plastic utensils, napkin, natural raffia, foot warmer) **Finished sizes: invitation 4½" x 10¾", utensil cup 3" diameter x 3½" height, favor 3¾" x 6"**

SUPPLIES: *Cardstock:* (white) *Patterned paper:* (Gold Die Cut from Lucky collection) Creative Café; (Ring Around The Rosie from Play collection) American Crafts *Accents:* (white library pocket) Bazzill Basics Paper; (felt flowers) Creative Café; (orange brad) Heidi Swapp *Stickers:* (Sweater alphabet) American Crafts *Fibers:* (green striped ribbon) Scrapworks; (orange twine) *Font:* (Attic Antique) www.oldfonts.com *Other:* (yarn skein, knitting needles) **Finished sizes: invitation wrap 4" x 6", favor pocket 3½" x 5"**

⁙5⁙ Knitting Party Designer: Kim Kesti

INVITATION ❶ Trim patterned paper to finished size. ❷ Print invitation on cardstock, trim, and adhere. ❸ Wrap invitation around yarn skein. Attach felt flower with brad.

FAVOR POCKET ❶ Adhere patterned paper inside library pocket. ❷ Adhere patterned paper to pocket front. ❸ Affix stickers. Adhere ribbon. ❹ Tie felt flower with twine; adhere. Insert knitting needles.

W rap up yummy snacks for after school, a hike, or a long trip with these bag toppers, boxes, tins, and more. There's even a plate that little ones can decorate and fill with Santa's cookies.

SNACKS

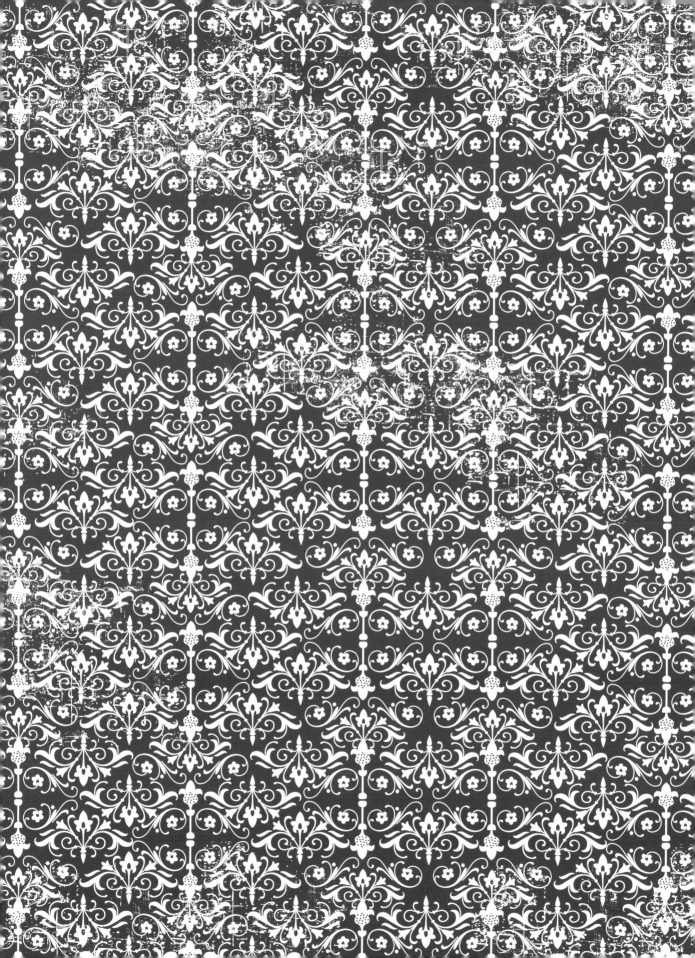

Oatmeal Chocolate Chip Cookies Brandy Jesperson

Several years ago I made these cookies for our new neighbors as a housewarming gift. They liked the treat so much they came over the next day asking for the recipe!

INGREDIENTS

2 sticks margarine
1 c. brown sugar
1 c. white sugar
2 eggs
1 tsp. vanilla
2½ c. flour
1 tsp. baking powder
1 tsp. baking soda
½ tsp. salt
2 c. oatmeal
1 bag chocolate chips

DIRECTIONS Mix first five ingredients. Add remaining ingredients. Roll dough into small balls and bake at 350 degrees for 8 to 10 minutes.

SUPPLIES: *Patterned paper:* (White Line Background) Scenic Route *Color medium:* (black pen) *Accents:* (arrow die cuts) Scenic Route; (vintage letter card) *Stickers:* (Small Block alphabet) Heidi Swapp *Fibers:* (black floral ribbon) American Crafts *Adhesive:* (decoupage) Plaid; (foam tape) *Other:* (black box) Provo Craft **Finished size: 7¼" x 5" x 3"**

Administrative Professionals Day Box Designer: Layle Koncar

❶ Adhere patterned paper to box lid and sides. ❷ Detail die cuts with pen; adhere. ❸ Adhere card with foam tape. Spell "Thank" with stickers. ❹ Write sentiment with pen. Tie ribbon.

Cookies for Santa Plate & Place Mat

Designer: Brandy Jesperson

PLATE ❶ Spell sentiment with stickers. ❷ Apply rub-ons. ❸ Draw lines, dots, and detail stockings with markers; adhere rhinestones.

PLACE MAT ❶ Attach transparency sheet to cardstock with brads. ❷ Adhere rhinestones.

DESIGNER TIPS

• Transparencies are great for place mats because they are waterproof and easy to clean.

• Creating a plate for Santa is a great "Mommy and me" project. Have your little ones help affix the stickers and after it is completed they can display it at home until Christmas Eve.

SUPPLIES: *Cardstock:* (red) *Transparency sheet:* (Vintage Wallpaper) Hambly Screen Prints *Color medium:* (green, black markers) Sanford *Accents:* (clear rhinestones) Darice; (green rhinestones) Doodlebug Design; (silver brads) *Rub-ons:* (stockings) American Crafts *Stickers:* (Cheeky Shimmer alphabet) Making Memories *Other:* (ivory plate) IKEA **Finished sizes: plate 9¾" diameter, place mat 12" x 10"**

Microwave Peanut Brittle Kim Kesti

A quick, easy recipe, handed down from my grandmother back when microwaves were "new fangled" appliances. It's so yummy, too.

INGREDIENTS

1 c. sugar
½ c. corn syrup
1 c. salted peanuts
1 tsp. vanilla
1 tsp. butter
1 tsp. baking soda

DIRECTIONS Microwave sugar and corn syrup in bowl for 4 minutes on high. Add peanuts, microwave on high for 4 more minutes. Add vanilla and butter; microwave 1 minute on high. Add baking soda to make mixture bubble. Stir and pour into greased pan; let cool. Break into bite-sized pieces.

5 STEPS Recipe Box & Cards

Designer: Linda Beeson

RECIPE BOX ❶ Cut patterned paper to fit box lid and sides; ink edges and adhere. ❷ Cut patterned paper to fit inside box; ink edges and adhere.

DIVIDERS ❶ Cover with patterned paper; ink edges. ❷ Punch scallop circles from patterned paper; adhere. ❸ Stamp desired image on cardstock, watercolor, and punch out. Ink edges and adhere.

CARDS Stamp from the kitchen of and recipe.

DESIGNER TIP

Remember to lightly sand items you want to alter, especially if the surface is glossy. Paper will adhere better if you sand first.

OUTSIDE

SUPPLIES: *Cardstock:* (white)
Patterned paper: (Heart Strings, Honey from Hey Sugar collection) Cosmo Cricket *Rubber stamps:* (from the kitchen of, recipe, baked with love, yummy stuff, oven, cupcake, muffin from Baked With Love set) Cornish Heritage Farms *Dye ink:* (Coal Black) Clearsnap *Chalk ink:* (Chestnut Roan, Warm Red) Clearsnap *Color medium:* (red, brown, peach, pink, yellow watercolor crayons) Dick Blick Art Materials *Adhesive:* (decoupage) Plaid *Tools:* (scallop, 2" circle punches) Marvy Uchida; (water brush) Sakura *Other:* (wood box, recipe cards, dividers)
Finished sizes: box 9" x 7½" x 7 1/4", dividers 8" x 6½", cards 8" x 5"

SUPPLIES: *Cardstock:* (Crimson) Bazzill Basics Paper *Patterned paper:* (Swirl/Red, Stripe/Dot, Tree/Green from Season's Greetings collection) Pebbles Inc. *Chalk ink:* (Chestnut Roan) Clearsnap *Accents:* (holly brads) Heidi Grace Designs; (red rhinestones) Doodlebug Design; (olive eyelet) We R Memory Keepers *Stickers:* (kraft labels, sentiment tiles) Making Memories *Fibers:* (cream velvet rickrack) Maya Road; (red/white striped ribbon) *Adhesive:* (foam tape) *Other:* (can) Crate Paper **Finished sizes: can 3" diameter x 6¼" height, card 3¾" x 5¼"**

✦5✦ Christmas Treat Can & Card Designer: Melissa Phillips

Ink paper edges.

CAN ❶ Cover can with patterned paper. ❷ Adhere patterned paper strip. Adhere patterned paper to lid. ❸ Affix label sticker to cardstock; trim. ❹ Set eyelet, attach brad, and adhere rhinestones. Affix tile sticker. ❺ Adhere rickrack. Tie tag to can with ribbon.

CARD ❶ Make card from cardstock. Cover with patterned paper. ❷ Adhere patterned paper square and strip. ❸ Adhere rickrack. ❹ Affix label sticker to cardstock; trim. Attach brad, adhere rhinestones, and affix tile sticker. ❺ Adhere label to card with foam tape.

Corn Pop Candy Stacy Croninger

This recipe was given to me years ago. At that time, you could only find corn pops around Christmas. Now these puffy corn pieces are available year-round.

INGREDIENTS

1 large bag corn pops (found on the chip aisle)
3 cubes butter
1½ c. sugar
5 tbsp. white corn syrup
5 tbsp. water

DIRECTIONS Pour corn pops in a large bowl; set aside. In saucepan, mix remaining ingredients. Bring to a boil; boil for 4 minutes. Pour over corn pops; stir until completely coated. Cool and serve. These can be stored in an airtight container for several days.

SUPPLIES: *Cardstock:* (white, black) *Patterned paper:* (Baseball Stripe) Adornit-Carolee's Creations *Stickers:* (Roosevelt Jr. alphabet) American Crafts; (baseball circle) Adornit-Carolee's Creations *Fibers:* (black stitched ribbon) Making Memories *Dies:* (star, star circle, Varsity numbers) QuicKutz *Tools:* (die cut machine) QuicKutz; (⅛" circle punch) *Other:* (kraft paper bag, juice bottle) **Finished sizes: bag 5¼" x 7¾", juice bottle wrap 8½" x 2¾"**

Baseball Treat Bag & Juice Bottle Wrap Designer: Jennifer Miller

BAG ❶ Adhere patterned paper to bag. ❷ Fold bag top; adhere cardstock strip. Affix baseball circle sticker. ❸ Spell name with stickers.

JUICE BOTTLE WRAP ❶ Cut patterned paper to fit around bottle; mat with cardstock and adhere. ❷ Die-cut star circle from cardstock; adhere to lid. ❸ Die-cut star from cardstock; mat with cardstock. ❹ Die-cut numbers from cardstock; adhere. ❺ Punch and tie to bottle with ribbon.

DESIGNER TIP

When mass producing, keep your project simple so that your last project looks as good as your first.

⦂5⦂ Funky Popcorn Holder Designer: Ana Cabrera

① Punch two circles from cardstock. **②** Trim transparency sheet to desired height x 12". **③** Cut slits each ¼" along one long edge of transparency strip to form tabs; fold in. Adhere tabs to cardstock circle. Adhere strip ends together. Adhere cardstock circle to holder bottom. **④** Affix fabric tape. **⑤** Adhere patterned paper strip.

SUPPLIES: *Cardstock:* (kraft) *Patterned paper:* (Pink Bohemian) Hambly Screen Prints *Transparency sheet:* (Mini Graph) Hambly Screen Prints *Sticker:* (black fabric tape) Making Memories *Tool:* (3" circle punch) **Finished size: 3¾" diameter x 3¾" height**

Granola Joy Candrian

I got this recipe when my children were really small. Over the years we've tweaked it, but my now-grown children all love it whether it's warm from the oven or cold with milk. We also like it sprinkled on yogurt or in a baggy for a healthy snack on the run.

INGREDIENTS

10 c. old-fashioned oats
½ c. sunflower seeds
1 c. brown sugar
1 tsp. salt
2 tsp. cinnamon
1 c. whole wheat flour
⅓ c. wheat germ
1 c. chopped nuts
2 c. coconut
1 c. honey
⅓ c. oil
1 tsp. vanilla
1 cube melted butter

DIRECTIONS In large bowl, stir together the first 9 ingredients. Add remaining ingredients. Mix, pour into a large baking pan at least 10" x 13", bake at 350 degrees, stirring every 5 minutes for 20 to 25 minutes or until light brown. Once it's cooled, store in large resealable plastic bags.

BOX ❶ Cover inside and outside of box with patterned paper; sand edges. ❷ Ink chipboard frame; adhere patterned paper behind frame. Adhere to box. ❸ Adhere chipboard letters. ❹ Die-cut airplane and sailboat from patterned paper; adhere pieces together. Adhere to box. *Note: Adhere with foam tape where needed.*

SEWING CARDS ❶ Die-cut sailboat, airplane, train, truck, and car from chipboard and patterned paper; adhere together. ❷ Punch outside edges.

SPOOLS ❶ Die-cut spools from chipboard and patterned paper; adhere together. ❷ Cut slits to secure yarn ends; wrap yarn around spools.

BAG TOPPER ❶ Make topper from patterned paper. ❷ Adhere patterned paper strip. Adhere border die cut. ❸ Cut train from patterned paper; adhere with foam tape. ❹ Die-cut "Chew-chew" from patterned paper; adhere.

SUPPLIES: *Patterned paper:* (Going, Fast, Traffic, Wheels, Freeway, Stoplight from Zoom collection) Crate Paper *Dye ink:* (Ruby Red) Stampin' Up! *Accents:* (chipboard alphabet, border die cut) Crate Paper; (chipboard frame) Technique Tuesday *Fibers:* (red, brown, green, blue yarn) Uniek *Adhesive:* (foam tape) 3M *Dies:* (sailboat, airplane, train, truck, car, spool, Plantin Schoolbook alphabet) Provo Craft *Tools:* (die cut machine) Provo Craft; (⅛" circle punch) *Other:* (wood cigar box) Darice; (chipboard) **Finished sizes: box 8¾" x 8¾" x 1¾", sewing cards approx. 6¾" x 5¾", spools 1¾" x 2¾", bag topper 6" x 2½"**

SUPPLIES: *Cardstock:* (brown, green) *Patterned paper:* (Sumner Kraft Tree) Scenic Route *Color medium:* (black pen) *Stickers:* (nature, hole reinforcer) Scenic Route *Fibers:* (brown stitched ribbon) *Font:* (Pharmacy) www.dafont.com **Finished sizes: invitation 8¾" x 5½", tag 3¾" x 1¾"**

Great Outdoors Hiking Party Designer: Layle Koncar

INVITATION ❶ Cut cardstock to finished size. Adhere patterned paper. ❷ Print sentiment on cardstock; trim and adhere. ❸ Adhere ribbon. Trim leaves from patterned paper; adhere. ❹ Write party information on back.

TAG ❶ Cut tag from cardstock; punch hole. ❷ Adhere stickers. Write "Enjoy!". ❸ Thread ribbon.

Special K Treats Brenda Peterson

This is a quick throw-together recipe that is great for summer road trips or a simple family picnic.

INGREDIENTS

1 c. sugar
1 c. corn syrup
1 c. peanut butter
6 c. Special K cereal
1 pkg. (6 oz.) chocolate chips
1 pkg. (6 oz.) butterscotch chips

DIRECTIONS In saucepan, bring sugar and corn syrup to boil and quickly mix in peanut butter and Special K. Spread mixture into 9" x 13" pan. Melt chocolate chips and butterscotch chips; pour over top of mixture. Cool and cut into squares.

SUPPLIES: *Cardstock:* (white, black) *Digital elements:* (lined patterned paper, swirls/circles rub-ons, frame from Graphic Garden No. 01 kit; black paper from Jaded kit; Grimey alphabet brushes from Grace kit; brain brush from Label Me Sane set) www.designerdigitals.com *Font:* (Indie Star BB) www.fontfinder.ws *Software:* (photo editing) *Other:* (tin) Maya Road **Finished size: 5¼" x 6¼" x 3"**

Brain Food Tin
Designer: Terri Davenport

❶ Create 4¾" x 4½" project in software. Drop in patterned paper. ❷ Add rub-ons and frame. ❸ Place paper behind frame. Brush brain; type "Feed me!". Add circle. ❹ Spell "Brain food" with alphabet brushes. ❺ Print on cardstock; trim. Adhere to cardstock and adhere to tin.

DESIGNER TIP
Create a new layer for each letter in the title, allowing you to resize or move letters as needed without affecting the others.

BONUS IDEA
Replace the brain image with a test-taking checklist. Include items such as "Get a good night's sleep", "Study hard", etc., on the list. Be sure to include "Eat well" and circle it.

My Hero Treat Can
Designer: Linda Beeson

1 Adhere patterned paper to can sides and lid; sand edges.
2 Cover chipboard star with patterned paper. Adhere tag behind star; trim and adhere. **3** Spell "My hero" on tag with rub-ons. Affix stickers. Tie tag to handle.

SUPPLIES: *Patterned paper:* (Scallop Stars & Stripes, Liberty Stars, Glory Stripes, Oh My Stars from Star Spangled collection) Paper Salon *Accents:* (chipboard star) Paper Salon; (distressed tags) American Tag *Rub-ons:* (Rummage alphabet) Making Memories *Stickers:* (star, word label) Paper Salon *Adhesive:* (decoupage) Plaid *Other:* (white round can) **Finished size: 6¾" diameter x 5¼"**

Crispy Cereal Mix Courtesy of AllRecipes.com

This great cereal mix is another version of the favorite crispy cereal party mix that everyone loves!

INGREDIENTS

6 tbsp. margarine
2 tbsp. Worcestershire sauce
¾ tsp. garlic powder
1½ tsp. seasoning salt
½ tsp. onion powder
1 c. mixed nuts
1 c. mini pretzels
1 c. bagel chips
3 c. crispy corn cereal squares
3 c. crispy rice cereal squares
3 c. crispy wheat cereal squares

DIRECTIONS Preheat oven to 250 degrees. Melt margarine in 9" x 13" baking pan. Remove baking pan from oven. Stir in Worcestershire sauce, garlic powder, seasoning salt, and onion powder. Gradually mix in nuts, pretzels, bagel chips, crispy corn cereal squares, crispy rice cereal squares, and crispy wheat cereal squares. Evenly coat all ingredients. Bake approx. 1 hour. Drain on paper towels.

Thinking of You Tag

Designer: Lindsey Botkin

① Make tag from patterned paper. ② Adhere cardstock strip. Ink tag edges. ③ Apply rub-ons. Stamp sentiment. ④ Adhere flower die cut; trim. Adhere circle die cut with foam tape. ⑤ Attach eyelet and knot with ribbon.

SUPPLIES: *Cardstock:* (white) *Patterned paper:* (Splendid from Sweet Branch collection) Crate Paper *Clear stamp:* (sentiment from All Occasions set) Inkadinkado *Solvent ink:* (Timber Brown) Tsukineko *Accents:* (silver eyelet) Making Memories; (flower, circle die cuts) Crate Paper *Rub-ons:* (circles border, butterfly) Crate Paper *Fibers:* (brown grosgrain ribbon) May Arts *Adhesive:* (foam tape) **Finished size: 6" x 2¾"**

SUPPLIES: *Cardstock:* (Ruby Slipper, Beetle Black, Rusted, Nutmeg, Bazzill White, Tiara shimmer) Bazzill Basics Paper *Dye ink:* (Basic Black) Stampin' Up! *Accents:* (black eyelets) Making Memories *Font:* (CK Corral) Creating Keepsakes *Dies:* (sword, pirate skull, ship) Provo Craft *Tool:* (die cut machine) Provo Craft **Finished size: 7" x 3¾"**

5 STEPS Enjoy, Matey! Bag Topper Designer: Wendy Gallamore

❶ Make bag topper from cardstock; ink edges. ❷ Cut squares from cardstock; adhere. ❸ Die-cut sword, pirate skull, and ship from cardstock; adhere pieces together and adhere to bag topper. ❹ Print sentiment on cardstock; trim, ink edges, attach eyelets, and adhere.

Warm up the hearts of your loved ones with these hot and savory homemade soups and stews, and coordinating paper-crafted projects. Whether you're making these tasty meals and pretty projects for a wintry day, a Sunday dinner, to give away, or simply to feed your own family, they're sure to bring a smile to your friends and loved ones' faces.

SOUP

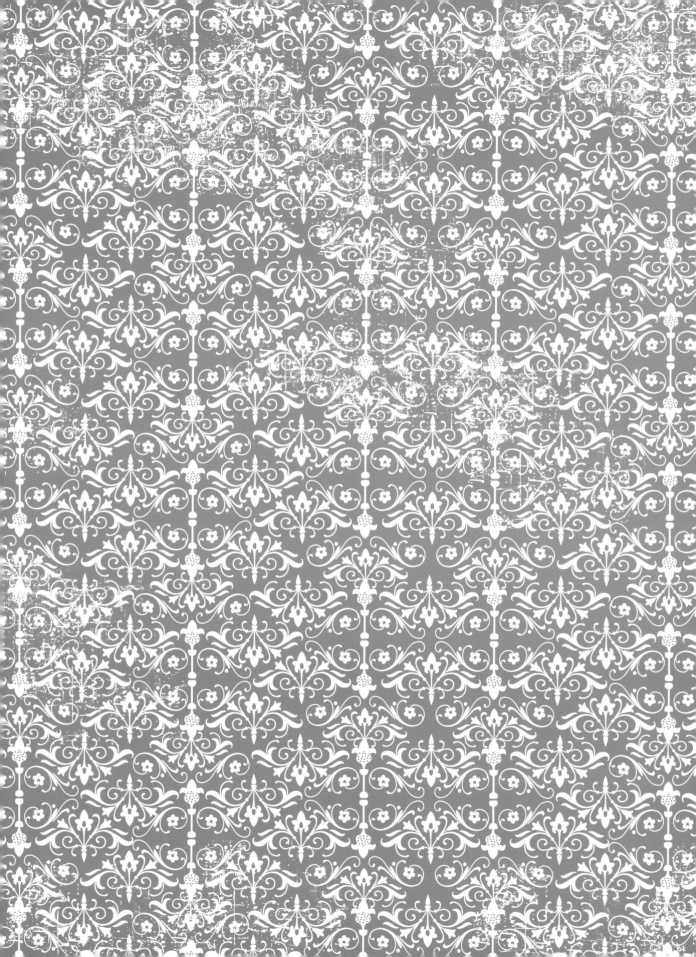

Chicken Curry Soup Celeste Rockwood-Jones

My Jordanian neighbor is a fabulous cook and has generously taught anyone interested in learning how to cook middle-eastern cuisine. This recipe is a hybrid of things I've learned from her, as well as an attempt to create something similar to my husband's favorite soup at a local Indian restaurant.

INGREDIENTS

2 leeks
3 tbsp. olive oil
2 lbs. boneless, skinless chicken breasts
2-3 potatoes, peeled and cubed
8 c. chicken broth
3 dried bay leaves
Salt and pepper to taste
Curry powder to taste
1 c. heavy cream
2-3 c. pre-cooked rice

DIRECTIONS Chop leeks (white portion) and sauté in olive oil in large pot about 5 minutes on medium heat. Add chicken (cut in bite-sized chunks), potatoes, and salt and pepper. Continue to sauté another 5 minutes or so. Add chicken broth and bay leaves. Cook covered on medium heat for 20 minutes. Add rice, curry powder, and cream. Simmer uncovered for 20 minutes, stirring occasionally. *Note: For thicker soup, add more rice. For a coconut flavor, add 2 cans of coconut milk in place of the cream.*

SUPPLIES: *Cardstock:* (blue, gold, white) *Patterned paper:* (Somerset from Wild Woodland collection) Tinkering Ink *Accents:* (gold, blue rhinestones) Westrim Crafts *Font:* (Samarkan) www.dafont.com *Other:* (clear cellophane bag, cooking spice) **Finished sizes: invitation 4¼" x 5½", bag topper 5" x 2¾", place cards 3¾" x 3¾"**

5 STEPS Curry Over for Dinner Ensemble   Designer: Alisa Bangerter

INVITATION ❶ Make card from cardstock. ❷ Cut rectangle of patterned paper. Adhere. ❸ Print "Dinner" on cardstock; trim and adhere. ❹ Cut strip of cardstock. Adhere. ❺ Adhere rhinestones.

BAG TOPPER ❶ Repeat invitation steps 1-2. ❷ Print "For you" on cardstock; trim and adhere. ❸ Repeat invitation steps 4-5. ❹ Fill cellophane bag with spice; staple bag topper to bag.

PLACE CARDS ❶ Repeat invitation steps 1-2. ❷ Print guest name on cardstock; trim and adhere. ❸ Repeat invitation steps 4-5. ❹ Repeat steps to make additional place cards.

Warms My Heart Tag Celeste Rockwood-Jones

1 Print sentiment on cardstock. Trim, following pattern on p. 176. **2** Punch hole in tag. Apply glitter. **3** Cut leaves from felt, following pattern on p. 176; apply glitter to edges. **4** Cut flower from felt, following pattern on p. 176. Adhere flower to leaves; adhere button. **5** Fill jar with soup. Tie ribbon around jar. Attach tag and adhere felt accent.

SUPPLIES: *Cardstock:* (light purple glossy) *Accents:* (purple glitter) Martha Stewart Crafts; (purple button) *Fibers:* (purple/burgundy ribbon) *Font:* (Filosofia Unicase) www.myfonts.com *Other:* (white, pink felt; craft jar, soup) **Finished size: 4" x 5" x 4"**

Potato Corn Chowder Brenda Peterson

I enjoy making this recipe in the fall when it is getting cold outside. It makes me feel warm and toasty.

INGREDIENTS

¼ c. butter
1 c. onion, chopped
1 clove garlic, minced
1 rib celery, chopped
2 – 3 c. potatoes, diced
¼ c. flour
1 can whole corn
1 can (4 oz.) chopped green chilis
1 can chicken broth
2 c. milk
Salt and pepper to taste

DIRECTIONS Sauté onion, garlic, and celery in butter until limp. Stir in corn with liquid and chilis. Sauté for 3 minutes. Boil potatoes until tender. Combine all other ingredients except milk and flour. Mix. Stir milk and flour until dissolved and heated through, but not boiling. Serve hot.

YIELDS 4-6 SERVINGS

INVITATION _Ink all paper edges._ ① Make card from cardstock. Cover with patterned paper. ② Print maze on cardstock. Trim, mat with cardstock, and adhere. ③ Print "You're invited" on cardstock. Trim into tag and punch hole. Set aside. ④ Print "Start" and "Finish" on cardstock. Trim and adhere to maze. Adhere raffia. ⑤ Wrap ribbon around card front. Attach tag with floss and foam tape.

CENTERPIECE _Ink all paper edges._ ① Cut strip of patterned paper; wrap around jar and adhere. ② Wrap ribbon around jar and knot. Cut notch in ends of ribbon. ③ Print "Happy fall y'all!" on cardstock. Trim and mat with cardstock. Attach brad. ④ Adhere piece to dowel to make sign. ⑤ Fill jar with popcorn. Fill pie pan with crackers. Set jar inside pie pan. Insert sign.

FAVOR ① Cut length of ribbon. Thread through whistle and adhere ribbon ends together. ② Print guest name on cardstock. Trim into tag and ink edges. Punch hole. ③ Attach tag to whistle with raffia.

SUPPLIES: _Cardstock:_ (Aloe Vera, Light Fawn) Bazzill Basics Paper; (yellow) _Patterned paper:_ (Father Knows Best from Picklelicious collection) Rusty Pickle _Dye ink:_ (Coffee Bean) Paper Salon _Accents:_ (copper brad) Making Memories _Fibers:_ (yellow polka dot ribbon, natural raffia) Michaels; (light green floss) _Font:_ (Blue Highway) www.dafont.com _Adhesive:_ (foam tape) _Tools:_ (⅛", ¹⁄₃₂" circle punches) _Other:_ (glass jar, wood dowel, whistle, pie pan, popcorn, crackers) **Finished sizes: invitation 5" square, centerpiece 9" diameter x 10" height, favor 14¾" long**

SUPPLIES: All supplies from Making Memories unless otherwise noted. *Patterned paper:* (Audrey Polka Dot Stripe, Ava Loopy Stripe from Noteworthy collection) *Accent:* (burgundy glitter chipboard frame) *Stickers:* (glitter flowers) *Fibers:* (cream lace) *Font:* (LB Jaimi) Creating Keepsakes **Finished size: 5½" x 4¾"**

5 STEPS Bloomin' Blossoms Card Designer: Wendy Sue Anderson

❶ Make card from patterned paper. Cut rectangle of patterned paper; adhere and stitch edges. ❷ Adhere lace. ❸ Print "Get well" on patterned paper. Trim sentiment to match frame; adhere behind frame. Adhere finished piece to card. ❹ Affix stickers.

DESIGNER TIP

Apply additional adhesive to the stickers prior to affixing them to ensure they'll stay securely in place.

Italian Sausage & Tortellini Soup Alice Golden

I love to cook and experiment with different recipes to come up with something new. This recipe was based in part on a recipe given to me by my son's second grade teacher, Mrs. Sullivan. I also used to make another soup with spinach, tortellini, and beef broth that was pretty good, too. When I combined our favorite elements from both soups into this recipe it became our new favorite.

INGREDIENTS

1 tbsp. olive oil
1 lb. sweet Italian sausage (or pork, chicken, or turkey sausage)
4 large carrots, sliced about ¼" thick on the diagonal
1 large onion, chopped
3 large cloves of garlic, minced
1 large green pepper, diced into ½" pieces
2 small zucchini, sliced in half and then cut into half rounds
3–4 handfuls of baby spinach
1 tsp. dried thyme
1 tsp. dried basil
1 can (14.5 oz.) stewed tomatoes
4 c. beef stock
2 c. water
1 bag frozen tortellini
2 tbsp. lemon juice
Salt and pepper to taste

DIRECTIONS Heat oil in large soup pot over medium heat. Remove casings from sausage and add sausage to pot. Allow to start to get brown and then use a wooden spoon to "cut" them into bite-sized chunks. Once sausage is fairly well browned, add onions and cook for 5 minutes or until soft, and then add garlic and cook for an additional 30 seconds or so until fragrant. Add carrots, green pepper, zucchini, thyme, and basil, and sauté for another minute or two. Add tomatoes, beef stock, and water, and bring to a boil. Reduce heat and simmer for 30 minutes, or until vegetables are tender.

In a separate pot, parboil tortellini for about 3 to 4 minutes; drain and add to soup, then simmer for another 15 to 30 minutes until tortellini are fully cooked. Just before serving, add the spinach, cover the pot, and let it cook for another minute or two. Season with salt and pepper, and stir in lemon juice. Serve with crusty bread.

SUPPLIES: *Cardstock:* (white) *Patterned paper:* (Clover Dot from Double Dot collection) Bo-Bunny Press *Transparency sheet; Rubber stamp:* (lips from Sweet Celebrations set) Hanna Stamps! *Dye ink:* (Real Red, Old Olive) Stampin' Up! *Paint:* (Wicker White, Licorice) Plaid *Accent:* (iridescent glitter) Stampin' Up! *Fibers:* (black gingham ribbon) Offray *Font:* (Unnamed Melody) www.filecart.com *Adhesive:* (decoupage) Plaid; (foam tape) *Die:* (scalloped oval) Spellbinders *Tools:* (die cut machine) Provo Craft; (perforating tool) Stampin' Up!; (embossing stylus, ½" circle punch, corner rounder punch) *Other:* (wood sign) Walnut Hollow; (gift box with mirror) Creative Imaginations; (lipstick, breath mints) **Finished sizes: invitation 5½" x 4¼", sign 14" x 6", kiss kit 3¼" x 2½" x 1"**

Under the Mistletoe Party Designer: Jessica Witty

INVITATION ❶ Make tri-fold card from patterned paper, scoring at 4¼" and 8½". Round card front corners. Paint edges. ❷ Print "Meet me...under the mistletoe" on transparency sheet using mirror setting on printer. Trim sentiment in half. Rub sentiment pieces on card front and bottom flap. ❸ Tie ribbon around card and knot. ❹ Die-cut oval from cardstock; roll perforating tool across middle. Stamp lips on oval. Adhere to front flap. ❺ Print party information on cardstock. Trim, ink edges, and adhere inside.

SIGN ❶ Paint sign with black paint; apply white paint to edges. Cut patterned paper to desired fit; paint edges and adhere. ❷ Print sentiment on transparency sheet using mirror setting on printer. ❸ Trim sentiment and lay on sign; rub to transfer. ❹ Tie ribbon around sign and knot. ❺ Cut leaves and stems from patterned paper. Ink edges. ❻ Draw leaf veins with embossing stylus. Shape stems. Insert leaves/stems into ribbon knot. ❼ Punch three circles from cardstock; apply glitter. Adhere to leaves using foam tape.

KISS KIT

Outside ❶ Paint box; let dry. ❷ Cover lid with patterned paper. Paint box edges. ❸ Print "Kiss kit" on transparency sheet. Trim and rub to transfer to box top. ❹ Stamp lips.

Inside *Paint all paper edges.* ❶ Cover inside box lid and bottom with patterned paper. Tie ribbon around lid and knot. ❷ Paint mirror edges; adhere. ❸ Place lipstick and breath mints in box.

INSIDE

INSIDE

⁙5⁙ Italian Place Setting Designer: Wendy Johnson

PLACE MAT ❶ Cut place mat from patterned paper. Double-mat sides with cardstock. ❷ Tie ribbon around journaling circle sticker; affix. ❸ Print "Buon Appetito" on cardstock. Trim and mat with cardstock. Adhere. ❹ Adhere patterned paper behind frame. Trim and adhere.

NAPKIN RING ❶ Cut patterned paper to fit frame; adhere. ❷ Adhere ribbon.

CANDLE WRAP ❶ Adhere journaling label. ❷ Wrap ribbon around candle and knot. ❸ Print "Buona sera" on cardstock. Trim and adhere. ❹ Wrap strip of patterned paper around ribbon knot.

SUPPLIES: *Cardstock:* (black, green, red, white) *Patterned paper:* (Set the Table, Les Poulets, Salt & Pepper from French Kitchen collection) Reminisce *Accents:* (metal frames) EK Success *Stickers:* (journaling label, circle) Reminisce *Fibers:* (green grosgrain ribbon) Michaels *Font:* (Amienne) www.myfonts.com *Other:* (red candle) **Finished sizes: place mat 14¾" x 9", napkin ring 2" square, candle wrap 3¾" x 3¾"**

Mexican Bean Soup Alice Golden

I call this my paper crafting soup! Whenever I have major deadlines, I pull out the crock pot and make this yummy soup. This soup is based on a bunch of different recipes that I played around with until I came up with this version. One of my favorite things about this recipe is that it takes less than 5 minutes to make.

INGREDIENTS

1 can (15 oz.) pinto beans
1 can (15 oz.) kidney beans
1 can (15 oz.) navy beans
1 can (15 oz.) corn
1 can (28 oz.) diced tomatoes
1 can (15 oz.) Ro-tel or tomatoes with green chilis added
1 packet taco seasoning
½ packet dry ranch salad dressing
½ c. water

DIRECTIONS Place all ingredients in slow cooker; stir together. *Note: Do not drain canned items, include the liquid in the soup.* Cook on low for 6 to 8 hours. Serve with grated cheese, sour cream, and tortilla chips.

Dinner in a Basket
Designer: Melissa Phillips

CAN WRAPS ① Cover can in cardstock. ② Cut strip of patterned paper slightly smaller than can. Adhere. ③ Affix stickers on tag to spell can contents. ④ Thread jute through tag and wrap around can; tie. ⑤ Attach brad to felt flower. Adhere. ⑥ Repeat steps to make additional can wraps.

RECIPE CARD ① Print soup recipe on cardstock. Trim and double mat with patterned paper and cardstock. ② Punch hole in card. Attach flower to card with brad.

Mexican Bean Soup

1 15 OZ. CAN OF PINTO BEANS
1 15 OZ. CAN OF KIDNEY BEANS
1 15 OZ. CAN OF NAVY BEANS
1 15 OZ. CAN OF CORN
1 28 OZ. CAN OF DICED TOMATOES
1 15 OZ. CAN OF RO-TEL OR TOMATOES
        WITH GREEN CHILIS ADDED
1 PACKET TACO SEASONING
1/2 PACKET DRY RANCH SALAD DRESSING
1/2 C. WATER

SUPPLIES: *Cardstock:* (Aztec) Bazzill Basics Paper; (cream) *Patterned paper:* (Blue Swirls, Brown Pixies, Décor Stripe from Wild Saffron collection) K&Company *Accents:* (aqua, copper glitter brads) Making Memories; (red, green, gold tags) Creative Café; (blue, orange, brown felt flowers) American Crafts *Stickers:* (Pure Type alphabet) Mustard Moon *Fibers:* (jute) *Font:* (Old Type) www.twopeasinabucket.com *Other:* (basket, cans of soup, can of chilis) **Finished sizes: large can wrap 10" x 4¾", small can wrap 9" x 2¾", recipe card 4½" x 3½"**

Grandma D's Beef Soup Cath Edvalson

The funny thing about this recipe is that I don't ever remember my Grandma D preparing this stew—just my mom. When I make it for my own family, it reminds me of cold winter Sundays back in my hometown of Ogden, Utah.

INGREDIENTS

2 – 3 tbsp. vegetable oil
2 lbs. beef cubes
1 onion, sliced
4 c. boiling water
1 tbsp. salt
1 tbsp. lemon juice
1 tsp. sugar
1 tsp. Worcestershire sauce
½ tsp. paprika
2 bay leaves
¼ tsp. allspice
6 carrots, sliced
1 lb. pearl onions
4 potatoes, cubed
2 stalks celery, sliced

DIRECTIONS Brown beef and onion in vegetable oil. Add boiling water and seasonings. Cover and simmer for at least 2 hours. Add vegetables and cook for 30 minutes more. Thicken with cornstarch, if desired.

SUPPLIES: *Cardstock:* (Swimming Pool) Bazzill Basics Paper; (white) *Patterned paper:* (Musical Chairs, Disco Ball, Cocktail from Celebration collection) American Crafts *Accents:* (green brads) Making Memories *Stickers:* (chipboard glitter alphabet) Doodlebug Design *Font:* (Jacks BV) www.chank.com *Tools:* (1", 2", 2½", 3" circle punches; decorative-edge scissors) *Other:* (clear cellophane bag) Nashville Wraps **Finished sizes: treat bag topper 5" x 3¾", award badge 3" x 6¼", invitation 6¾" x 5½"**

Snowman Building Party Designer: Kim Kesti

TREAT BAG TOPPER ❶ Print "Just for", "Thanks for coming!", and dotted box on cardstock. Trim and fold into bag topper. ❷ Trim strip of patterned paper with decorative-edge scissors; adhere to inside edge of bag topper. ❸ Affix stickers to spell "You". ❹ Punch circle of patterned paper; adhere inside "o". ❺ Attach brads. ❻ Fill bag with desired contents. Attach bag to bag topper with stapler.

AWARD BADGE ❶ Print "Place winner" and dotted box on cardstock; trim. ❷ Trim strip of patterned paper with decorative-edge scissors; adhere to reverse side of badge. ❸ Punch three circles from patterned paper and cardstock. Trim one with decorative-edge scissors. Layer and adhere circles to badge. ❹ Affix stickers to spell "1st".

INVITATION ❶ Print invitation text and dotted box on cardstock; trim. ❷ Trim strip of patterned paper with decorative-edge scissors; adhere to reverse side of invitation. ❸ Spell "Snowman" with stickers. Punch circle of patterned paper. Adhere inside "o". ❹ Attach brads.

⁙5⁙ Hits the Spot Thermos Tag Designer: Alice Golden

❶ Print "Hope this hits the spot!" on patterned paper. Trim into tag. Apply rub-ons. ❷ Mat tag with cardstock. Punch hole. ❸ Attach charm to tag with trim.

SUPPLIES: *Cardstock:* (Sage Dark) Prism *Patterned paper:* (Big Game Hunting from Hunting Season collection) Karen Foster Design *Accents:* (pewter binoculars charm) Karen Foster Design *Rub-ons:* (bullseye, scope, shots) Karen Foster Design *Fibers:* (brown suede trim) *Font:* (Tasklist) www.twopeasinabucket.com **Finished size: 3" x 7¼"**

Minestrone Soup with Parmesan Crumble Susan Neal

On a cold winter's night, this is the perfect, hearty main dish soup. The Parmesan Crumble adds texture and zest!

SOUP INGREDIENTS

2 tbsp. olive oil
2 tbsp. butter
½ lb. Italian sausage (use spicy if you like it hot)
1 large onion, chopped
2 cloves garlic, minced
1 c. carrots, chopped
1 c. celery, chopped
2 tbsp. dried Italian seasoning
Salt and pepper
1 can (28 oz.) stewed tomatoes, chopped
4 c. chicken stock
1 c. zucchini, chopped
½ c. frozen thawed spinach, chopped or
2 c. fresh, chopped
1 can (19 oz.) red kidney beans with liquid
¾ c. small pasta (elbow macaroni, mini rigatoni, or tubetti)

DIRECTIONS Heat olive oil and butter in large soup pot. Cook Italian sausage (remove from casing), break up with spatula or spoon into smaller pieces. When almost fully cooked, add onion, carrots, and celery. Cook, stirring for approximately 5 minutes until onion is soft. Add garlic and sauté another 2 minutes. Add seasonings and rest of ingredients. Simmer for 10 minutes. Ladle into bowls.

PARMESAN CRUMBLE INGREDIENTS

1 c. grated parmesan
2 c. bread crumbs
1 tbsp. Italian seasoning
¼ c. butter

DIRECTIONS Melt butter in a sauté pan until lightly brown. Add remaining ingredients and sauté until well incorporated. Sprinkle over soup.

Harvest Party
Designer: Julia Stainton

PLACE MARKERS ❶ Make place marker from cardstock. Ink edges. ❷ Stamp guest name and desired image. Wrap ribbon around place marker front; adhere. ❸ Stamp desired image on cardstock; punch into circle and ink edges. Mat with punched cardstock circle; adhere. Thread button with floss and adhere or attach brad. ❹ Repeat steps to make additional place markers.

BASKET TAG ❶ Make tag from cardstock. Ink edges of patterned paper; adhere. Zigzag-stitch edges. ❷ Set eyelet in tag. ❸ Punch two squares from cardstock, one slightly larger. Stamp pumpkin and sentiment; ink edges. Mat with punched square and adhere to tag. Thread button with floss

and adhere. ❹ Punch circle from cardstock. Ink edges. Bend circle slightly, using tag side. Adhere to back of tag. ❺ Attach tag to basket with ribbon.

INVITATION ❶ Make card from cardstock. ❷ Stamp cardstock with Burlap Backgrounder; trim and adhere. Ink edges of patterned paper; adhere. Stitch around piece. ❸ Stamp large leaf and sentiment on cardstock; punch into circle and ink edges. Mat with punched cardstock circle; adhere. ❹ Adhere bird. Thread button with floss and adhere. ❺ Attach brads.

SUPPLIES: *Cardstock:* (Birchtone Dark, Spring Willow Medium, Natural Smooth) Prism; (kraft) Stampin' Up!; (cream) *Patterned paper:* (North Street from Sumner collection) Scenic Route *Rubber stamps:* (large leaf, small leaf, sunflower, acorn, pumpkin from Fall Silhouettes set; Burlap Backgrounder; sentiment from Let's Get Stuffed set; Quirky alphabet) Cornish Heritage Farms *Dye ink:* (Pumpkin Pie, Old Olive, Chocolate Chip, More Mustard, Ruby Red, Basic Black) Stampin' Up! *Accents:* (black brads) Creative Impressions; (brown corduroy brad) Imaginisce; (red, orange, yellow buttons) Daisy D's; (felt bird) Maya Road; (gold eyelet) *Fibers:* (black/cream ribbon) May Arts; (tan floss) Stampin' Up! *Tools:* (1½", 1¾" circle punches) EK Success; (square punches) *Other:* (basket) Michaels **Finished sizes: place markers 3" x 2", basket tag 2½" x 3½", invitation 5½" x 4¼"**

SUPPLIES: *Cardstock:* (ivory) *Patterned paper:* (Ripe from Mellow collection) BasicGrey; (Holiday Cheer, First Gift from Wonderland collection) Cosmo Cricket; (Donna from Vintage Holiday collection) Melissa Frances *Rubber stamp:* (tag from Majestic Reverie Mini set) Inque Boutique *Pigment ink:* (Cocoa, Dune, Merlot) Clearsnap *Accents:* (brown, yellow, green buttons) Autumn Leaves *Fibers:* (copper ribbon) Michaels; (white floss) DMC; (white lace trim) *Font:* (Batik Regular) www.themeworld.com *Adhesive:* (foam tape) *Tools:* (decorative-edge scissors, corner rounder punch) **Finished sizes: card 5" square, tag 2¾" x 4½"**

⁙⁵ₜₑₚₛ Away from Home Card & Tag Designer: Anabelle O'Malley

ACCENT PIECE ❶ Cut two squares from cardstock and patterned paper. Round corners, ink edges, layer, and adhere. ❷ Cut soup bowl and steam from patterned paper, following pattern on p. 175. Adhere.

CARD ❶ Make card from cardstock. Cut slightly smaller piece of patterned paper. Ink edges and adhere. ❷ Cut square of patterned paper; ink edges. Mat edges with patterned paper; trim with decorative-edge scissors and adhere. ❸ Cut square of patterned paper. Ink edges and adhere. ❹ Print "A taste of home" on cardstock. Trim, ink edges, and adhere. ❺ Adhere trim. Thread buttons with floss and adhere. ❻ Adhere accent piece with foam tape.

TAG ❶ Make tag from patterned paper. Cover with patterned paper piece and strip; ink edges. Mat with cardstock. ❷ Stamp tag on patterned paper. Trim and adhere. Adhere trim. ❸ Cut hearts from patterned paper. Ink edges and adhere. ❹ Print soup name on cardstock. Trim, ink edges, and adhere. ❺ Adhere ribbon loop and button. Thread button with floss and adhere.

French Onion Soup au Gratin Susan Neal

Easy, cheesy, and perfect for a dinner party.

FRENCH SOUP INGREDIENTS

8 c. yellow onions (approx. 8 small onions), halved and thinly sliced
½ c. sliced shallots
2 cloves garlic, minced
½ c. butter
Fresh thyme, approximately 2 tsp. leaves (or ½ tsp. dried thyme)
¼ c. brandy or cognac
½ c. Madeira, sherry, or red wine
1 bay leaf
6 c. beef broth or homemade stock
Salt and pepper

DIRECTIONS Cook onions and shallots on low heat in butter until soft (approx. 20 minutes). Add garlic and thyme. Continue to cook for 10 minutes on a slightly higher heat to caramelize onions (they will turn golden brown). Deglaze pan with brandy. Cook a minute until liquid is almost all evaporated. Add sherry, broth, bay leaf, and seasonings. Simmer for 30 minutes.

Preheat oven to 450 degrees. Place ovenproof soup bowls on a jelly roll sheet pan. Ladle soup into bowls.

GRATIN TOPPING INGREDIENTS

2 c. grated Gruyere cheese (can substitute Emmentaler, Fontina, Jarlsberg, Gouda, or Swiss—basically anything that melts well and is flavorful)
French bread, cut into pieces (approximately ½")
Olive oil

DIRECTIONS Place French bread pieces on cookie sheet. Drizzle with a little olive oil and toss. Bake in 400 degree oven until dry and slightly toasted. Place in soup bowls and top with approximately ½ c. cheese. Cook for about 10 minutes until cheese is golden and bubbly.

SUPPLIES: *Cardstock:* (ivory) *Patterned paper:* (Clayton Street from Ashville collection, Kincaid Ave from Sumner collection) Scenic Route *Dye ink:* (Van Dyke Brown) Ranger Industries *Color medium:* (Chocolate pen) EK Success *Accents:* (silver head pins, clear crystal beads) www.jewelrysupply.com; (leaf glass beads) Blue Moon Beads *Font:* (Ympyroity) www.dafont.com *Tool:* (oval punch) *Other:* (jump rings, wire hoops) www.jewelrysupply.com **Finished sizes: invitation 4¾" x 8¾", wine bottle tag 3" x 6", wineglass charms ¾" x 1½"**

5 STEPS Wine Tasting Party   Designer: Layle Koncar

INVITATION ❶ Make invitation from patterned paper. ❷ Print invitation information on cardstock, leaving 3" space at top. Trim, ink edges, and adhere. ❸ Cut leaves from patterned paper. Adhere. ❹ Write "Wine tasting party" on invitation, using pen.

WINE BOTTLE TAG ❶ Make tag from cardstock. Punch oval. ❷ Write year and wine contents on tag front, using pen. ❸ Ink edges. ❹ Cut leaves from patterned paper; adhere. Attach tag to bottle.

WINEGLASS CHARMS ❶ String two beads on wire hoop. ❷ String leaf glass bead on head pin. Make loop at end of pin; cut excess. *Note: Bend at right angle away from bead.* ❸ Attach piece to hoop with jump ring.

SUPPLIES: *Cardstock:* (pink, cream, white) *Patterned paper:* (Silver Damask) Daisy D's *Rubber stamp:* (Eiffel Tower from Paris Ephemera set) Art Declassified *Pigment ink:* (Silver) Clearsnap *Embossing powder:* (clear) Ranger Industries *Accents:* (tags) Uline *Fibers:* (pink grosgrain ribbon) May Arts *Dies:* (Opposites Attract alphabet) Provo Craft *Tool:* (die cut machine) Provo Craft **Finished sizes: card 5½" x 5½", favor 3½" x 5¼"**

Merci Dinner Card & Favor Designer: Teri Anderson

CARD ❶ Make card from cardstock. ❷ Mat edge of patterned paper square with cardstock. Adhere. ❸ Attach ribbon to tag and knot. Adhere. ❹ Stamp and emboss Eiffel Tower on cardstock. Trim and adhere to tag. ❺ Die-cut "Merci" from cardstock; adhere.

FAVOR ❶ Cut two pieces of cardstock to finished size. Adhere on three sides to form pocket. ❷ Adhere cardstock and patterned paper strips. ❸ Attach ribbon to tag and knot.

Adhere. ❹ Stamp and emboss Eiffel Tower on cardstock. Trim and adhere to tag. ❺ Die-cut "For you" from cardstock; adhere.

W hip up sauces, mixes, and more with fresh, fun packaging to indulge your family and friends.

MISCELLANEOUS

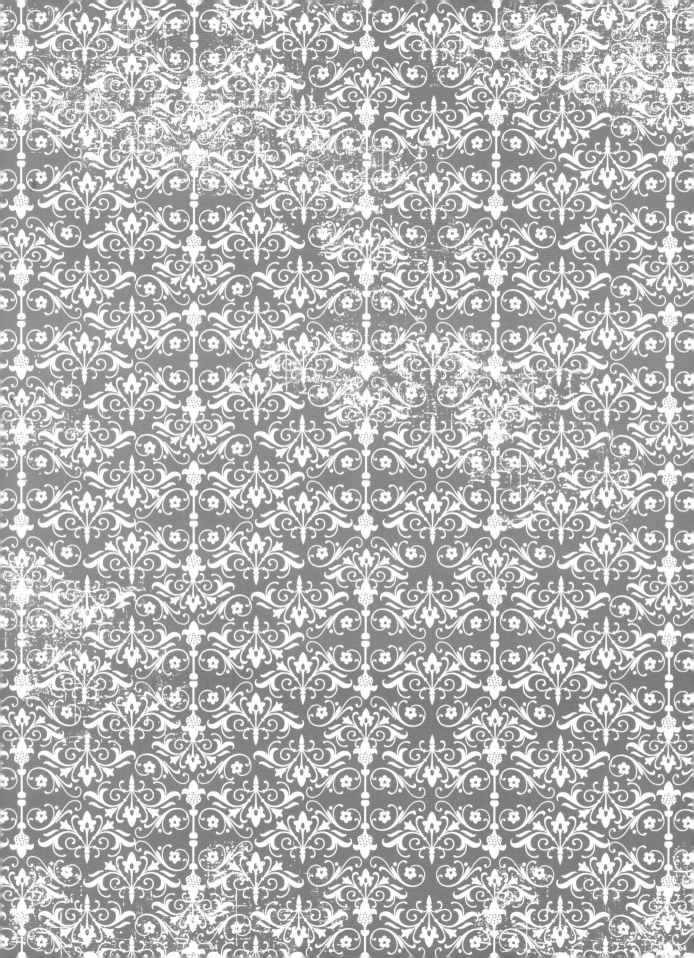

Spicy Mango Salad Dressing Brandy Jesperson

This sweet and spicy dressing is great for a summer salad, and with its fresh ingredients, it's great for your waistline, too.

INGREDIENTS

1 large mango, peeled, seeded, and chopped
⅓ c. seasoned rice vinegar
¼ c. lime juice
3 tbsp. brown sugar
1 tbsp. almond oil
2 green onions, minced
1 clove garlic, minced
½ tbsp. ginger, minced
¼ tsp. salt
Black pepper to taste

DIRECTIONS Combine ingredients. Chill until ready to use or serve at room temperature.

SUPPLIES: *Cardstock:* (black) *Patterned paper:* (Masquerade from Elegant collection) American Crafts *Vellum:* (green) *Clear stamp:* (wreath from Winterland set) Inkadinkado *Dye ink:* (white) *Fibers:* (green cording; black grosgrain, green polka dot ribbon) *Tools:* (1" scalloped circle punch) Martha Stewart Crafts; (2", 1½", ⅛" circle punches) *Other:* (jar) **Finished size: 3¾" diameter x 6¾" height**

Festive Neighbor Gift Jar Designer: Celeste Rockwood-Jones

❶ Cut patterned paper to fit around jar; adhere. ❷ Wrap ribbon around jar; adhere. Wrap ribbon around jar; knot. ❸ Punch circle from cardstock; stamp wreath. Punch hole and attach to ribbon with cording. ❹ Punch scalloped circle from patterned paper and circle from vellum. Layer circles; adhere to lid.

BONUS IDEA
Create a coordinating recipe card.

Jamaican Jerk Marinade Brandy Jesperson

I love this marinade on grilled chicken—it's the perfect dish for a backyard barbeque with family and friends.

INGREDIENTS

1 jalapeno pepper, seeded and diced
3 tbsp. water
2 tbsp. lime juice
2 tbsp. lemon juice
1 tbsp. Dijon mustard
4 cloves garlic, minced
2 cubes chicken bullion
½ tsp. ground cumin
¼ tsp. dried thyme

DIRECTIONS Combine ingredients in airtight container. Pour marinade over 1 lb. chicken or desired meat; let sit in fridge 4 hours. Remove meat from marinade; heat remaining marinade. Cook meat on grill until done, basting periodically with heated marinade.

DID YOU KNOW?

- When marinating, use a glass, plastic, or ceramic container; metal containers can chemically react with the acidic ingredients and cause an unpleasant taste.

- Marinate in the refrigerator; never at room temperature.

- Heat or discard any remaining marinade.

- Marinated meat can be grilled, broiled, stir-fried, sautéed, or even baked.

SUPPLIES: *Cardstock:* (white) Bazzill Basics Paper; (Giallo) Prism *Patterned paper:* (Board Short from Vibe collection) Creative Imaginations; (Dad & Me Blue from Celebrate collection) My Mind's Eye *Clear stamp:* (sun from Garden Icons set) KI Memories *Dye ink:* (Lemonade) KI Memories *Accents:* (white paper flower) American Crafts; (blue, orange paper flowers) Prima; (yellow brads) Bo-Bunny Press; (yellow eyelet) Provo Craft; (metal-rimmed tags) Avery *Fibers:* (orange grosgrain ribbon) American Crafts *Fonts:* (CK Surfer, CK Sassy, CK Vegas Nights) Creating Keepsakes *Adhesive:* (foam tape) Mrs. Grossman's *Tool:* (1¼" circle punch) Family Treasures *Other:* (craft sticks) **Finished sizes: invitation 4½" x 8", tag 3¼" x 6¾", food pick 2½" x 5"**

5 STEPS Taste of the Caribbean BBQ Party
Designer: Dee Gallimore-Perry

INVITATION ❶ Make card from cardstock. ❷ Cut patterned paper slightly smaller than card front; adhere. ❸ Print party details on cardstock; trim. ❹ Adhere patterned paper strips. Attach flowers with brads. ❺ Adhere block to card.

TAG ❶ Make tag from patterned paper; mat with cardstock. ❷ Print recipe name and sentiment on cardstock; trim. ❸ Adhere patterned paper strip. Attach flower with brad; adhere block to tag. ❹ Set eyelet; thread with ribbon.

❺ Stamp sun on white; punch circle. Adhere to tag. ❻ Adhere stamped tag with foam tape.

FOOD PICKS ❶ Print menu item on cardstock; trim. Double-mat with patterned paper. ❷ Cut patterned paper to fit printed block; place craft stick between pieces and adhere. ❸ Stamp sun on cardstock; punch circle. Adhere to tag. ❹ Adhere stamped tag with foam tape.

SUPPLIES: *Cardstock:* (Kraft) DMD, Inc.; (Rosey) Bazzill Basics Paper *Patterned paper:* (Heart Strings from Unconditional Love collection) My Mind's Eye *Rubber stamps:* (Winnie the Pooh alphabet) EK Success *Chalk ink:* (Chestnut Roan) Clearsnap *Accents:* (pewter eyelet) We R Memory Keepers; (letter stencil) Chartpak; (black paper clips) *Fibers:* (jute) *Fonts:* (Vintage) www.twopeasinabucket.com *Tool:* (file tab punch) McGill *Other:* (jar with lid) **Finished size: 3½" x 4½"**

Jamaican Jerk Marinade Tag Designer: Nicole Keller

Ink and distress all paper edges. ❶ Make tag from patterned paper. Set eyelet. ❷ Adhere cardstock behind stencil and attach paper clip. Adhere to tag. ❸ Stamp "Amaican erk marinade" on patterned paper; trim and adhere. ❹ Print recipe on cardstock and stamp "Recipe"; trim. ❺ Punch file tab from patterned paper, fold, and adhere to recipe card. Attach paper clip. Adhere recipe card inside tag. *Note: Adhere card with tape for easy removal.* ❻ Wrap jute around jar, thread through eyelet, and knot.

Inside 165

Hawaiian Coconut Syrup
Joy Candrian

Since my family loves anything tropical, this syrup has been a winning topping for hot waffles, French toast, or pancakes. The first time I ever tried coconut syrup in Honolulu in 1971, I was hooked. This syrup is easy and quicker to make than a trip to the islands—although I truly prefer a trip to Hawaii.

INGREDIENTS

½ c. butter
1 c. sugar
½ c. buttermilk
½ tsp. baking soda
½ tsp. coconut extract

DIRECTIONS Melt butter in sauce pan; add sugar and stir until dissolved. Add buttermilk; boil 1 minute. Add baking soda and coconut extract; stir until combined. Serve warm with chopped macadamia nuts, sprinkled coconut, or sliced bananas for an extra-special treat.

BOX *Stitch all paper edges.* ❶ Paint box and lid. ❷ Trim patterned paper to fit around box; adhere. Cover lid with patterned paper. ❸ Adhere patterned paper strip to lid. ❹ Thread ribbon through slide; knot. Adhere to lid. ❺ Paint chipboard swirl and flower; add glitter. Adhere to box. ❻ Tie ribbon to swirl.

GIFT BAG ❶ Cut patterned paper slightly smaller than bag front; stitch edges. ❷ Tie ribbon around piece; knot. Adhere piece to bag. ❸ Trim flower clusters from patterned paper; adhere. ❹ Cut label from cardstock; stitch edges and adhere. ❺ Trim circle with heart from patterned paper; adhere. ❻ Spell "Pancake mix" with stickers. ❼ Paint chipboard

flowers; add glitter. Thread ribbon ends through flowers and knot.

TAG ❶ Make tag from patterned paper; stitch edges. ❷ Trim flower cluster from patterned paper; adhere. ❸ Affix sticker; zigzag-stitch edges. ❹ Tie ribbon around tag; knot. ❺ Paint chipboard heart and flower; add glitter and adhere.

JAR *Stitch all paper edges.* ❶ Trim patterned paper to fit around jar; adhere. ❷ Cut label from cardstock; adhere. ❸ Spell "Syrup" with stickers. ❹ Tie ribbon around jar; knot. ❺ Trim patterned paper to fit lid; adhere. ❻ Adhere ribbon around lip of lid.

SUPPLIES: *Cardstock:* (Kraft) Bazzill Basics Paper *Patterned paper:* (Florence, Cecilia, Lillian, Anne) Melissa Frances *Paint:* (white) Delta *Accents:* (chipboard heart, swirl, flowers) Fancy Pants Designs; (iridescent glitter) Doodlebug Design; (silver ribbon slide) Li'l Davis Designs *Stickers:* (wedding sentiment) Melissa Frances; (Loopy Lou alphabet) Doodlebug Design *Fibers:* (white satin ribbon) Michaels *Other:* (box) Nicole Crafts; (kraft bag) Emma's Paperie; (jar with lid, spatula) **Finished sizes: box 8" x 3½" x 6½", gift bag 4¾" x 10", tag 3¾" x 5½", jar 2½" diameter x 5½" height**

Southern Pepper Jelly Ashley Butler

This recipe is special to me because it is made by my Mawmaw. Everyone loves her pepper jelly, but as a child I thought the name sounded disgusting. So, I didn't try it until I was an adult. But once I tried it, I discovered it has an unusually pleasing taste—a mix of sweet and peppery.

INGREDIENTS

¾ – 1 c. jalapeno peppers, seeded and finely chopped
1⅓ c. bell pepper, chopped
6½ c. sugar
1½ c. wine vinegar
6 oz. liquid pectin
Red food coloring, as desired

DIRECTIONS Combine peppers, sugar, and vinegar in large pot. Boil 1 minute. Reduce heat; cook 5 minutes, stirring constantly. Remove pot from heat. Add liquid pectin and food coloring; gently stir mixture. Pour into jars immediately. Wipe jar tops with wet towel before sealing.

YIELDS 8 JARS (8 OZ. EACH) *NOTE: COOKED JELLIES MAY BE STORED ON THE SHELF UNOPENED FOR 1 YEAR.*

SERVING SUGGESTIONS

- Serve the jelly over cream cheese and with crackers.
- Baste grilled meats.
- Mix with cream cheese until smooth and serve over ice cream.

DESIGNER TIPS

- Wear gloves when working with jalapeno peppers, or use a food processor to avoid potential eye irritation from the pepper juice.
- For best results, use Certo liquid pectin.
- Do not double the recipe, as it may not set.
- Use sterilized jars, lids, and utensils when preparing cooked jellies. Wash items in hot, soapy water and rinse. Place them in boiling water for 10 minutes and keep them in hot water until you're ready to use them.

TAG ① Make tag from cardstock. ② Cut flames, following pattern on p. 176; layer and adhere to tag. ③ Apply chalk to flames. ④ Print "Happy birthday" and "Stuff!" on cardstock; trim. Apply chalk; adhere to tag. ⑤ Spell "Hot" with stickers. Punch hole in tag; attach chain.

JAR WRAP ① Wrap jar with cardstock. ② Cut flames, following pattern on p. 176; layer, chalk, and adhere to jar.

SUPPLIES: *Cardstock:* (Bazzill Red, Apricot, Bazzill Yellow) Bazzill Basics Paper; (white, black) Provo Craft *Color medium:* (black chalk) Pebbles Inc. *Accents:* (silver bead chain) Making Memories *Stickers:* (Cheeky Shimmer alphabet) Making Memories *Font:* (CK Jolly Elf) Creating Keepsakes *Other:* (jar) Cost Plus World Market **Finished sizes:** tag 3¾" x 4¼", jar 2¼" x 4" x 1¾"

Sand Art Brownies Courtesy of AllRecipes.com

Mix the ingredients in a large jar in the same way kids make sand art today!

INGREDIENTS

⅔ c. all-purpose flour
¾ tsp. salt
⅓ c. unsweetened cocoa powder
½ c. all-purpose flour
⅔ c. brown sugar, packed
⅔ c. white sugar
½ c. semisweet chocolate chips
½ c. vanilla baking chips
½ c. walnuts

DIRECTIONS Layer ingredients in wide-mouth quart size jar in order listed. Create decorative tag with baking instructions.

TO USE: Preheat oven to 350 degrees. Grease 9" square pan. Pour jar contents into bowl; mix well. Add 1 tsp. vanilla, ⅔ c. vegetable oil, and 3 eggs; beat until combined. Pour batter into prepared pan. Bake in preheated oven for 25 to 30 minutes.

1 Make card from cardstock. **2** Adhere strip and rectangle of patterned paper. **3** Trim flowers from die cut paper with craft knife; adhere to card. *Note: Adhere one with foam tape.*

4 Adhere buttons. Adhere trim and tie twine around card; knot. **5** Stamp sentiment on cardstock; trim and adhere.

SUPPLIES: *Cardstock:* (natural, beige) DMD, Inc. *Patterned paper:* (Alleluia, Lucia from Yuletide collection) Tinkering Ink *Specialty paper:* (Flower Child Socialite die cut from Pop Culture collection) KI Memories *Clear stamps:* (alphabet) Target *Dye ink:* (Java Fizz) Ranger Industries *Accents:* (brown button) SEI; (cream button) *Fibers:* (hemp twine) Darice; (cream lace trim) *Adhesive:* (foam tape) **Finished size: 4" x 6"**

Chocolate Sauce Cindy Schow

This is a recipe I like to make and keep in the fridge for when I want a quick dessert. It's easy to make and has a nice rich chocolate flavor. Mmm...it makes me hungry just thinking about it!

INGREDIENTS

6 tbsp. butter
2 c. sugar
¼ c. cocoa
1 c. evaporated milk

DIRECTIONS Combine all ingredients in pot; boil 5 minutes. Remove from heat. Serve warm with vanilla ice cream, brownies, cake, or your favorite dessert.

Ice Cream Party
Designer: Alisa Bangerter

INVITATION ① Cut and tear ice cream cone pieces, following pattern on p. 175. Crumple scoop pieces; flatten and apply chalk. ② Score lines on reverse of cone piece; highlight with chalk. Adhere scoop pieces to cones. ③ Cut strip of cardstock, fold, and adhere ends to pieces to form card. ④ Adhere torn scoop piece with foam tape. ⑤ Apply dimensional glaze to sauce piece; let dry. Adhere. ⑥ Wrap ribbon around front cone; knot. Adhere button to bow. ⑦ Print "It's a party!" on cardstock; trim. Chalk edges, mat with cardstock, and adhere with foam tape.

JAR WRAP ① Cut rectangle from cardstock. ② Score lines on reverse side; highlight with chalk. ③ Tear strip of cardstock; crumple, flatten, and apply chalk. Adhere to base.

④ Punch holes; thread with ribbon, leaving excess length to tie around jar. Make bow and adhere button; adhere to ribbon. ⑤ Thread ribbon through buttons and card, leaving excess length. ⑥ Print "Chocolate ice cream sauce" on cardstock; trim. Chalk edges, mat with cardstock, and adhere with foam tape.

DESIGNER TIP

Use a computer mouse pad, ruler, and stylus to score lines to resemble the cross-hatching on an ice-cream cone.

SUPPLIES: *Cardstock:* (tan, brown, pink) *Color medium:* (brown, red chalk) Craf-T Products *Accents:* (pink buttons) Stampin' Up! *Fibers:* (pink/brown grosgrain, pink/white satin ribbon) May Arts *Font:* (CK Surfer) Creating Keepsakes *Adhesive:* (foam tape) Making Memories *Tools:* (⅛" circle punch) Fiskars *Other:* (dimensional glaze) Stampin' Up! **Finished sizes: invitation 4" x 6¾", jar wrap 7¾" x 3½"**

SUPPLIES: *Cardstock:* (Pansy Purple, Baby Pink) Close To My Heart *Patterned paper:* (Friendship Hearts from Girls Will Be Girls collection) Adornit-Carolee's Creations *Clear stamp:* (together from Friendship Word Puzzle set) Close To My Heart *Watermark ink:* Tsukineko *Embossing powder:* (White Daisy) Close To My Heart *Accents:* (metal-rimmed tag) Avery; (silver mini brad) Making Memories *Fibers:* (pink grosgrain ribbon) Offray *Fonts:* (Angelica) www.dafont.com; (Tall Pen) Close To My Heart *Tools:* (⅛",1" circle punches, corner rounder punch) **Finished size: 3½" x 6¾"**

So Sweet Together Tag Designer: Tresa Black

❶ Make tag from cardstock; round corners and distress edges. ❷ Print "Chocolate ice cream sauce" on cardstock; trim and adhere. ❸ Distress edges of patterned paper piece; adhere. Stamp together on cardstock; emboss. Trim, distress edges, and adhere. ❹ Attach ribbon loop to tag with brad. ❺ Print "So sweet" on cardstock, punch into circle, and adhere to metal-rimmed tag. ❻ Punch hole, tie with ribbon, and adhere to tag.

BONUS IDEA

Change the tag color scheme to coordinate with the container you use for the sauce. Or, use a clear glass container to show off the rich chocolate color of the sauce.

Patterns <small>Copy at 200%</small>

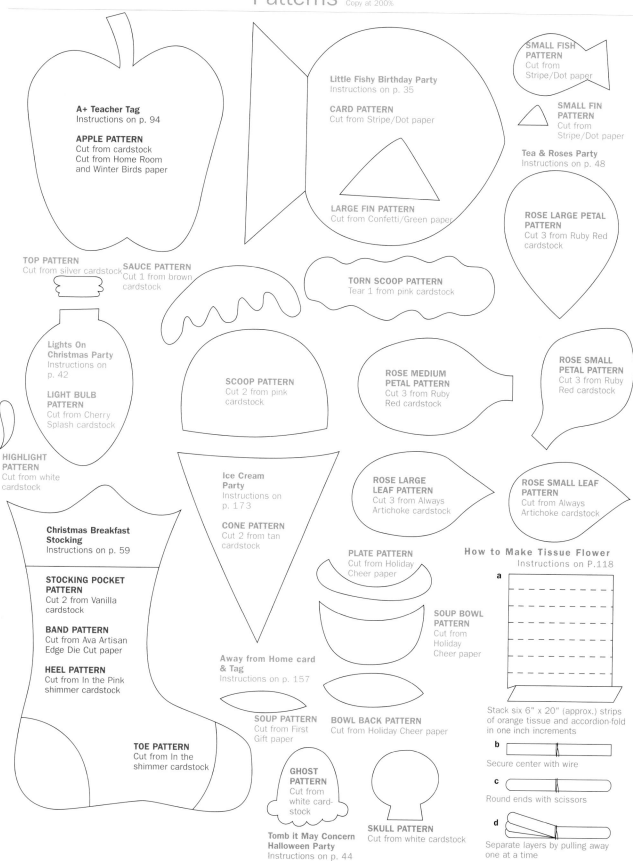

A+ Teacher Tag
Instructions on p. 94

APPLE PATTERN
Cut from cardstock
Cut from Home Room
and Winter Birds paper

Little Fishy Birthday Party
Instructions on p. 35

CARD PATTERN
Cut from Stripe/Dot paper

LARGE FIN PATTERN
Cut from Confetti/Green paper

SMALL FISH PATTERN
Cut from
Stripe/Dot paper

SMALL FIN PATTERN
Cut from
Stripe/Dot paper

Tea & Roses Party
Instructions on p. 48

ROSE LARGE PETAL PATTERN
Cut 3 from Ruby Red cardstock

TOP PATTERN
Cut from silver cardstock

SAUCE PATTERN
Cut 1 from brown cardstock

TORN SCOOP PATTERN
Tear 1 from pink cardstock

Lights On Christmas Party
Instructions on p. 42

LIGHT BULB PATTERN
Cut from Cherry Splash cardstock

SCOOP PATTERN
Cut 2 from pink cardstock

ROSE MEDIUM PETAL PATTERN
Cut 3 from Ruby Red cardstock

ROSE SMALL PETAL PATTERN
Cut 3 from Ruby Red cardstock

HIGHLIGHT PATTERN
Cut from white cardstock

Ice Cream Party
Instructions on p. 173

CONE PATTERN
Cut 2 from tan cardstock

ROSE LARGE LEAF PATTERN
Cut 3 from Always Artichoke cardstock

ROSE SMALL LEAF PATTERN
Cut from Always Artichoke cardstock

Christmas Breakfast Stocking
Instructions on p. 59

STOCKING POCKET PATTERN
Cut 2 from Vanilla cardstock

BAND PATTERN
Cut from Ava Artisan Edge Die Cut paper

HEEL PATTERN
Cut from In the Pink shimmer cardstock

PLATE PATTERN
Cut from Holiday Cheer paper

SOUP BOWL PATTERN
Cut from Holiday Cheer paper

How to Make Tissue Flower
Instructions on P.118

a

Stack six 6" x 20" (approx.) strips of orange tissue and accordion-fold in one inch increments

b

Secure center with wire

c

Round ends with scissors

d

Separate layers by pulling away one at a time

Away from Home card & Tag
Instructions on p. 157

SOUP PATTERN
Cut from First Gift paper

BOWL BACK PATTERN
Cut from Holiday Cheer paper

TOE PATTERN
Cut from In the shimmer cardstock

GHOST PATTERN
Cut from white cardstock

Tomb it May Concern Halloween Party
Instructions on p. 44

SKULL PATTERN
Cut from white cardstock

Patterns Copy at 200%

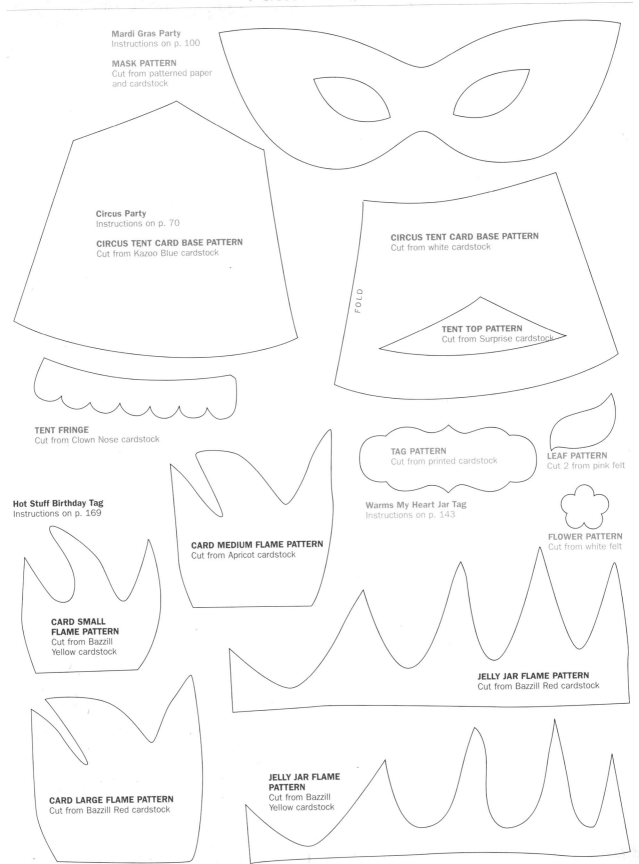

Mardi Gras Party
Instructions on p. 100

MASK PATTERN
Cut from patterned paper
and cardstock

Circus Party
Instructions on p. 70

CIRCUS TENT CARD BASE PATTERN
Cut from Kazoo Blue cardstock

CIRCUS TENT CARD BASE PATTERN
Cut from white cardstock

FOLD

TENT TOP PATTERN
Cut from Surprise cardstock

TENT FRINGE
Cut from Clown Nose cardstock

TAG PATTERN
Cut from printed cardstock

LEAF PATTERN
Cut 2 from pink felt

Hot Stuff Birthday Tag
Instructions on p. 169

Warms My Heart Jar Tag
Instructions on p. 143

FLOWER PATTERN
Cut from white felt

CARD MEDIUM FLAME PATTERN
Cut from Apricot cardstock

**CARD SMALL
FLAME PATTERN**
Cut from Bazzill
Yellow cardstock

JELLY JAR FLAME PATTERN
Cut from Bazzill Red cardstock

CARD LARGE FLAME PATTERN
Cut from Bazzill Red cardstock

**JELLY JAR FLAME
PATTERN**
Cut from Bazzill
Yellow cardstock